BI KU-524-746

CHANNEL
ISLANDS

1986/1987 Edition

By the staff of Berlitz Guides
A Macmillan Company

How to use our guide

- All the **practical information,** hints and tips that you will need before and during the trip start on page 110, with a complete rundown of contents on page 113.
- For **general background,** see the sections The Islands and the People, p. 6, and A Brief History, p. 15.
- All the **sights** to see are listed between pages 27 and 94, with suggestions for a day trip to France on pages 95 to 97. Our own choice of sights most highly recommended is pinpointed by the Berlitz traveller symbol.
- **Leisure activities** are described between pages 98 and 104, while information on **restaurants** and cuisine is to be found on pages 107 to 109.
- Finally, there is an **index** at the back of the book, pp. 127–128.

Although we make every effort to ensure the accuracy of all the information in this book, changes occur incessantly. We cannot therefore take responsibility for facts, prices, addresses and circumstances in general that are constantly subject to alteration. Our guides are updated on a regular basis as we reprint, and we are always grateful to readers who let us know of any errors, changes or serious omissions they come across.

Text: Ken Bernstein
Photography: Monique Jacot
Layout: Dominique Michellod
We wish to thank Mike Banfield of the States of Guernsey Tourist Board, and Stuart Abraham and Diane Needham of Jersey Tourism, for valuable assistance. We are also grateful to Rick Morris for his help in the preparation of this book.
Cartography: Falk-Verlag, Hamburg.

Contents

Cover picture: St. Peter Port, Guernsey.
Photo pp. 2–3: Rocquaine Bay, Guernsey.

The Islands and the People

The Channel Islands are flower-topped cliffs and broad sand beaches, shopping sprees and a whiff of France under the Union Jack. Isolated but easy to reach, they enjoy all the modern comforts. Yet life is simple, as in bygone days: streets are clean, crime rare, prices sensible, air fresh. Even the cows seem to be smiling.

Scattered across the yawning Gulf of St. Malo, the Channel Islands are the warmest and sunniest of the British Isles. They come in one colour—green —and all sizes from small to almost microscopic. The largest, Jersey, has an area of 45 square miles, one-fifth the size of the Isle of Man. Toward the lower end of the league, the feudal island of Sark is one-tenth the area of Bermuda. Several other Channel isles are even tinier.

But all of them become vastly bigger when the tide goes out. Some of the most fearsome tides in the world wash the Channel Islands; at spring tide the water can rise as much as 40 feet in a morning. At low tide dozens of square miles of the sea bed are revealed to sunbathers, shell collectors, sandcastle designers and scavenging gulls. In the ports, fleets of yachts and fishing boats are beached, helpless as overturned turtles until the sea returns.

The author of *Les Misérables*, Victor Hugo, exiled for years in Jersey and Guernsey, called the Channel Islands "pieces of France fallen into the sea and picked up by England".

A glance at the map confirms his metaphor. The islands are

Low tide beaches St. Aubin fleet; Guernseyman mends his tackle.

much closer to France than to England—geographically. In fact, until only a few thousand years ago, Jersey was connected to the French mainland; the first settlers *walked* there from Normandy. But when the last Ice Age ended, the melting glaciers drastically raised the sea level and the land bridge was submerged.

While geography and history provide an enduring French connection, the islands are devoutly British—as they have been for centuries. Don't be surprised to hear someone with a French name blurt out, "Jolly good, old chap!" Here old-fashioned British patriotism has outlasted the empire. Indeed, the Channel Islands claim to be the oldest component of the British Commonwealth after England itself. Ever since 1066, almost without a break, they have been loyal to the British crown.

But allegiance to the Queen doesn't mean obedience to the British Government. Selected British laws are observed but by no means all. The islands are not colonies, nor are they independent. The 130,000 islanders, though British, are not citizens of the United Kingdom.

These ambiguities keep outsiders slightly off balance and add spice to the island scene. They also contribute to prosperity: aloof from U.K. finances, Jersey and Guernsey have minted creative tax policies that are good for business. Although accepted as associate members of the European Community, the islands are able to avoid the scourge of Value Added Tax.

A basic income tax of 20 percent lures many tax exiles to settle in the archipelago. Their mansions are among the stately sightseeing bonuses. But not everybody can enjoy a tax holiday so close to the bright lights of London and Paris. Effectively, only genuine millionaires are welcome to become residents; the moderately rich need not apply.

The benign fiscal climate also accounts for the profusion of banks, trusts, offshore funds and little-known holding companies listed on rows of small brass plaques hardly bigger than calling-cards. If the money squirreled away in bank accounts in Jersey came from local sources only, each indigenous man, woman and child would have had to con-

A salesman's smile engages the passers-by at Guernsey market.

9

Cyclists reap the scenic reward on a sunny bluff overlooking rural Jersey and the Channel beyond.

tribute something approaching a quarter million pounds.

Like the tycoons, the ordinary tourists profit from the tax collector's wink. The little luxuries of life are far less expensive than at home. Drinkers and smokers revel in yester-year's prices, and provincial housewives soon become authorities on gems and French perfumes.

Shopping is only one of the pleasures of the islands. An ABC of fascinations would start at archaeology and architecture and reach all the way to witchcraft, yachting and zoology.

If the weather is fair, you can kick up the surf on one of the boundless beaches, or hike deep into the interior, through lush valleys. It's a pleasure to roam the sea cliffs, sniffing the wild fennel, thyme and heather, and spying the birds—the migrating red-necked phalarope, for example, or the nesting yellow wagtail.

A rainy day needn't be a washout. Both main islands have built ambitious leisure centres aimed at keeping the

struction of dozens of round towers.

In World War II even the historic forts were conscripted anew. The Channel Islands were occupied by the Germans, who reinforced the ancient castles and built new defences on the scale of the Maginot Line. The remnants, from machine-gun bunkers to echoing underground cities, are overrun by tourists and military historians alike.

Jersey seems to cherish its wartime forts, many restored as historic monuments. Guernsey lets nature camouflage most of them into grassy hillocks. Alderney, which must have more pillboxes per acre than any place in the world, would rather forget. In their attitudes to the war, as in almost everything else, the islands insist on their individuality.

The rivalry between the Channel Islands has been a fixture for centuries. But it was aggravated during the English Civil War, when Jersey and Guernsey enlisted on opposite sides. To this day, Jerseymen call Guernseymen donkeys, while Guernseymen call Jerseymen toads. (Alderney citizens are called cows, and Sarkese crows. Tourists, too, suffer a nickname; they are called grockles—derivation uncertain.)

whole family amused with sports, games and diversions under cover. Or you can stroll through a greenhouse where enchanting butterflies will flutter onto your outstretched hand. Or tour a museum of folk relics or a historic granite church.

The archipelago's sturdy granite tells the story of civilization, and beyond. Thousands of years ago a pagan society built magnificent tombs in the islands, then vanished. Medieval Englishmen recycled the same stones to create almost invincible fortresses. In the late 18th century, fear of the French neighbours inspired the con-

From the air, Jersey looks intensely green and fertile, a milk-and-honey land basking in the sun. Guernsey sparkles: greenhouse glass covers one-fifteenth of its entire area, but the rest is pasture surrounding likeable villages. Alderney, the windswept loner, appears a happy but haphazard prairie. Regardless of their size, all the islands are equipped with beaches even Caribbean connoisseurs might covet. And the ocean's blues and greens match any South Seas colour chart.

You will search in vain for a Channel Islands tourist authority; each bailiwick—Jersey and Guernsey—runs its own. But they agree on one aspect of policy: too many tourists, like too many millionaires, are bad for the environment. So they've put a lid on the number of hotel rooms. The only way more visitors can come is if they spread out beyond the main summer rush into the marginal seasons.

Aside from the sun and scenery, many tourists are drawn to the islands by the curious cultural background. For the British it's a chance to feel at home abroad. The place names have a French sound, but you don't have to convert a foreign currency; everyone speaks English, and an honest pint of beer is a bargain. The French come over to eavesdrop on the old-timers speaking ancient Norman patois. Gallic visitors appreciate the British bobbies, but tend to squint dubiously at pub menu boards announcing native delicacies like baked beans on toast, spaghetti and chips, or mince, tatties and swede.

Even so, the food can be counted among the considerable advantages of the islands. This is where the famous tomatoes and potatoes come from, and kiwi-fruit, too. And the creamy milk produced by those beautiful Jersey and Guernsey cows whips into a fine froth for heaping on the local strawberries. The seafood is as sumptuous as you'd expect, given the location, but it's not cheap.

Like fishermen everywhere, the Channel Islands seafarers grumble that it's hard to make a living these days. Their ancestors probably complained as much in the 16th century, when they sailed all the way to North America for cod. Today's fishermen still wear the distinctive rain-resistant sweaters. Naturally, each island insists on its own design. So shopping for a pullover is no pushover: you'll have to decide whether to buy a jersey or a guernsey.

Facts and Figures

Geography: Seventy-five square miles of islands (seven inhabited), isles and rocky reefs in the English Channel. Jersey, the largest island with 45 square miles, is the southern-most of the British Isles. The northernmost Channel Island, Alderney, is nearest to both England and France—only 8 miles from the coast of Normandy.

Population: 130,000. Most populous island, Jersey, has a permanent population of 76,000. Many inhabitants of the Channel Islands trace their roots to ancient Normandy, which ruled until the Middle Ages and left a long-lasting cultural legacy.

Major towns: St. Helier, Jersey (population about 30,000); St. Peter Port, Guernsey (about 16,000).

Government: The Channel Islands are British but not part of the United Kingdom. They are divided into two bailiwicks, Jersey and Guernsey. Each bailiwick has a lieutenant-governor appointed by and representing the British Crown, and a bailiff presiding over local government and judiciary. The bailiwicks' legislatures, or States, are elected. Each bailiwick has its own laws based on 13th-century Norman practice. The islands have local peculiarities in government; the most unusual is Sark, a feudal domain.

Economy: The main industries are agriculture—dairying and growing vegetables—and tourism. An increasingly significant economic area is international banking and finance.

Currency: Each bailiwick issues its own banknotes and coins, interchangeable locally with British currency.

Religion: There is an Anglican Church in each parish; Methodist and Catholic churches are also strongly represented.

Languages: English is spoken in all islands; older residents of some country areas still speak a Norman-French dialect.

Climate: Sunniest weather in the British Isles with moderate rainfall, mostly in winter.

A Brief History

At the Royal Guernsey Golf Club, duffers are handicapped not only by obstacles of stone and sand, but also by moving hazards. The intruders wandering across the fairways, sand-traps and greens include cows, bird-watchers, archaeologists and historians. The 18-hole course overlooking the ocean is riddled with prehistoric graves, 18th-century fortifications and World War II bunkers.

The archaeological equivalent of a hole in one was achieved in 1976 just alongside the 5th green: a triangular array of stones, 20 yards along the longest leg, was discovered beneath the gorse. Tools found at the "dig" date back to around 4000 B.C. The site is called Les Fouaillages, and experts rate it as one of the oldest structures in all of Europe.

Less sophisticated traces of human endeavour in the Channel Islands go back much further. A cave in Jersey, La Cotte de St. Brelade, is said to have been occupied over 100,000 years ago. In those days, Jersey was part of Normandy, a peninsula jutting from a peninsula; it didn't become a proper island until after the last Ice Age.

All over the archipelago pre-historic sites have been found in dozens of farmers' fields: these include dolmens (stone slabs arranged as tombs), menhirs (monumental stones, sometimes aligned as temples) and passage graves (tombs reached by tunnel). According to all this evidence, the Neolithic residents of the Channel Islands had the technology to move ten-ton stones, the skill to carve them and devotion enough to build imperishable monuments to their princes and their gods.

The islanders graduated from the Stone Age to the Bronze Age and then to the Iron Age, but did not leave any significant legacy behind them. The Romans may or may not have colonized the islands (opinion is divided) but they certainly passed through; undersea archaeologists are getting to the bottom of a Roman shipwreck in the harbour of St. Peter Port. Shipwrecks have always been a Channel Islands speciality.

Vikings Ho!

Little news has reached us from the Dark Ages, but it's certain that Christianity had been

Fantasies float past happy crowds at Jersey's Battle of Flowers.

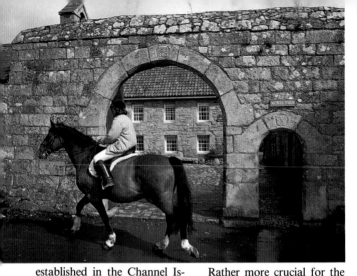

established in the Channel Islands by the 6th century. The first missionary to arrive in Guernsey, St. Sampson, went on to greater things as a bishop in Brittany. Jersey's St. Helier became a hermit on a rock in the harbour. He was martyred there, perhaps by visiting pirates, in the year 555.

Around the 9th century the Vikings came marauding. Later called Normans, these Norsemen finally gained control of Normandy from Charles the Simple of France. In the 10th century the sphere of influence of the Duke of Normandy expanded to include the Channel Islands.

Rather more crucial for the future of Europe, the Norman Duke William II (better known as William the Conqueror) went to war across the Channel. At the Battle of Hastings in 1066, he won the English crown. The Channel Islanders retained their allegiance to Normandy, but here began their long-standing association with the English crown.

Norman influences on life in the Channel Islands persist. The legal system remains essentially Norman; court officials still bear titles like *jurat* (a justice of the peace), *procureur* (prosecutor) and *greffier* (clerk). The land is still meas-

History in stone: a Jersey farmhouse and an ancient passage grave. Overleaf: Mont Orgueil Castle, overlooking peaceful port of Gorey.

ured in *perches* and *vergées*. If William the Conqueror were to visit the isles today he would probably understand the dialect spoken by the old people, though contemporary French speakers find it incomprehensible. Feudal society has changed least of all on the island of Sark, where the *Seigneur* (lord) is the only person allowed to own doves and a bitch.

England's hold over the Channel Islands turned the nearest neighbour, France, into a perennial threat. One of many attacks took place in 1214, by a French pirate disarmingly called Eustace the Monk, who set fire to whatever he could find. But many more massive French invasion forces were to come. At one time or another even the most formidable forts —Jersey's Mont Orgueil and Guernsey's Castle Cornet— were captured. Life under siege became so cruel that in 1483 Pope Sixtus IV issued a Papal bull proclaiming the Channel Islands neutral.

The Civil War

When civil war broke out in England, the Channel Islands were split down the middle. Guernsey joined the Parliamentary forces against the king, but Jersey was so fanatically loyal that the young Prince of Wales took refuge in Elizabeth Castle, St. Helier. He stayed for ten weeks, surrounded by several hundred retainers; even the crowd of uninvited guests couldn't damage his popularity with the islanders.

Three years later, when Charles I was beheaded, his son was again in Jersey. He was proclaimed King Charles II in St. Helier's Market Square. An understandably annoyed Oliver Cromwell decided to neutralize Jersey as a Royalist stronghold. An expeditionary force of Roundheads was despatched and soon overpowered the local militia.

Over in Guernsey, leading islanders needed little encouragement to join the Parliamentary cause at the outset of the civil war. The king had snubbed them in vital matters and appointed an unpopular governor. When Parliament took over, the governor and his supporters holed up in Castle Cornet. Besieged for more than eight years, they fired 30,000 cannon balls into Cromwell's St. Peter Port. In December 1651, the castle finally quit—the last Royalist bastion in the British Isles to surrender.

One of the most effective Cavaliers in Jersey, Sir George Carteret, was rewarded in 1664 by a grant of territory in the New World, between the Delaware and Hudson Rivers. He named it New Jersey.

Instant Justice

For more than a thousand years, any Channel Islands citizen has been able to get what amounts to an on-the-spot injunction, or restraining order, to stop an alleged injustice.

The wronged party invokes the *Clameur de Haro*, an ancient Norman cry for help. The complainant kneels before witnesses and cries: *"A l'aide, mon prince! On me fait tort''*. (Help, my prince! I am being wronged.) In some islands this must be followed by a recitation of the Lord's Prayer in French.

Although it's rare these days, islanders still claim the *Clameur* now and again, usually in the sort of dispute that blows up between neighbours. But the do-it-yourself restraining order is valid only until a court can rule on the case.

20

Industry and Defence

In the second half of the 17th century, peace brought prosperity, which spread from the local grandees to merchants, sailors and incipient industrialists. Privateering (legalized piracy) and smuggling swelled the archipelago's gross national product. To keep the "free trade" running, a sizeable shipbuilding industry developed; and hundreds of coopers were mobilized to manufacture barrels and kegs for the transshipment of duty-free (clandestine) wine and brandy.

New fields opened to agriculture. Apple orchards produced cider to slake a raging English thirst. Before Jersey and Guernsey cows became celebrities, the most important livestock on the islands were sheep. Knitting Channel Islands wool was such a lucrative hobby that everyone took it up—fishermen and farmers as well as women and children. To protect the rest of the economy, a moratorium on knitting had to be imposed during the harvests. The first big knitwear success was stockings. Much later it was discovered that the local fishermen's sweaters, jerseys and guernseys, respectively, were hot export items.

As tension with France heightened in the late 18th century, defence became a prime concern. Round forts, loosely called Martello Towers, were thrown up on all the coasts; dozens still stand. The militia was reinforced, but a French invasion at La Rocque, Jersey, in 1781, totally surprised the defenders. The lieutenant-governor, caught in bed, surrendered. But a local officer, Major Francis Peirson, refused to obey, engaging the French in a tumultuous battle in the very heart of St. Helier, in Royal Square. Both Peirson and the French commander, the Baron de Rullecourt, were mortally wounded, but Jersey triumphed. France never again attacked the Channel Islands.

Victorian Vitality

In the 19th century, nonetheless, the British government built comprehensive new fortifications throughout the islands to counter a French build-up. Two of the most controversial projects were huge breakwaters which still overpower the harbours of St. Catherine's Bay, Jersey, and Braye, Alderney. None of the islands reached the status of a Gibraltar, but thanks to the Admiralty's plan to dominate the Channel, the citizens began to enjoy modern ports, lighthouses, roads and railways.

With the introduction of regular steamship services, Channel Islands agriculture turned to perishable but profitable exports. Jersey new potatoes became a familiar delicacy in England, and the fruit of Guernsey greenhouses, originally grapes, then tomatoes, stormed the English market.

Queen Victoria made three ceremonial visits to the islands to inspect the improvements. Piers, towers, statues, schools and streets still named after Victoria and Prince Albert are reminders of those flourishing times.

Although Victoria's Channel Islands subjects were bursting with patriotism, few could speak—or even understand—the Queen's English. Ordinary islanders communicated in the ancient Norman patois. Formal occasions required French, the only language spoken in the Jersey legislature until 1899; Guernsey didn't get around to making English official until 1921. However, some older people still speak a Norman-French dialect.

Elegance of circular stone fortifications adds distinction to the coasts of the Channel Islands.

Channel at War

During World War II the islanders stoically endured five years of physical and psychological hardship.

When France fell to the Germans in 1940, Britain proclaimed the islands indefensible, the equivalent of an open city. Many islanders, including virtually the entire population of Alderney, fled to England, fearing the worst—which arrived soon enough. Thousands of German occupation troops swooped in. Hitler not only wanted to prevent Britain from using the islands, he saw them as a vital sector of his Atlantic Wall. Thousands of "slave workers" were imported to build impregnable command posts and gun emplacements.

Propaganda pictures of German troops goose-stepping past Lloyds Bank were just what Dr. Goebbels ordered. When the Allies started winning the struggle for Europe, Channel Islands civilians and occupying soldiers alike suffered extreme shortages of food, fuel and medicines. Late in the war, a Red Cross ship brought supplies that saved the islanders from disaster.

On May 9, 1945, the emaciated citizens put on their best clothes and gathered to listen to Winston Churchill broad- **23**

Landmark Events

100,000 B.C.	Hunters live in a Stone Age cave in Jersey, part of a peninsula still connected to mainland France. (It is cut off when the sea level rises, perhaps 3,000 B.C.)
5000 B.C.	Neolithic Guernseymen build a stone shrine at Les Fouaillages, on site of present-day golf course.
6th century	St. Sampson, a Welsh-born abbot, hermit and bishop, brings Christianity to Guernsey. St. Helier, son of Belgian nobles, carries the faith to Jersey.
9th century	Vikings win Normandy. As Normans, they take control of Channel Islands in 10th century.
11th century	William the Conqueror wins Battle of Hastings in 1066, becoming king of England; Channel Islanders shift allegiance to English sovereign.
13th century	French begin more than 200 years of attacks on British-ruled Channel Islands
14th century	Channel Islands besieged by French forces, who conquer Guernsey, Alderney and Sark.
15th century	Papal bull proclaims neutrality of Channel Islands, forbids Britain from building military bases.
16th century	Henry VIII orders fortification of Alderney. French Protestant refugees find sanctuary in Channel Islands. Elizabeth I grants feudal regime to ruler of Sark.
17th century	English Civil War splits the islands, which suffer attacks and sieges. Charles II proclaimed King in Jersey's Market Square. Postwar agriculture—and smuggling—thrive.
18th century	Islands build defensive towers as French threaten. Jersey militia overcomes invaders in final battle.
19th century	Steamships rush island produce to English markets. Queen Victoria inaugurates new ports and public works. Alderney is transformed into "Gibraltar of the Channel".
20th century	Germans occupy Channel Islands in World War II. Elaborate fortifications integrate islands into Hitler's "Atlantic Wall". Postwar prosperity is fuelled by tourism, intensive agriculture, and offshore banking.

casting the news of all-round German capitulation. Tears and cheers greeted his words: "And our dear Channel Islands are also to be freed today".

A Speedy Recovery
The German prisoners of war were immediately put to work dismantling forests of barbed wire and digging up more than 150,000 mines. Fortunately for all concerned, the methodical German army had posted *"Achtung!"* signs on the edges of mine-fields, and a particular colour of sign—known to all the islanders—always designated a field of decoys.

Less than a month after liberation, King George VI and Queen Elizabeth visited the islands to encourage the recovery programme. Soon afterwards, the evacuees were allowed to return and pick up the threads of their lives. The initial days of austerity passed swiftly, and tourism, high-powered agriculture and high finance brought unimagined prosperity to the islands.

After the dark days of World War II, the only belligerency acceptable is the Battle of Flowers. With typical rivalry, Jersey and Guernsey stage competing carnivals every August. In times past they wound up with altogether undignified flower-fights, hence the "battle" name. Tourists pour in to watch the the big parades, with millions of flowers decorating the carnival floats. The flowers provide a brilliant excuse for throwing a party. The islands have a lot to celebrate.

Bulwarks and Bunkers
The military history of the Channel Islands is so rich that souvenirs in stone fairly litter the coastline. The extraordinary clutter of bulwarks and bunkers may not be everybody's idea of a tourist attraction, but enthusiasts rave about the myriad of monuments. Even ordinary holiday-makers can catch the history bug.

Prehistory fans find the passage graves, menhirs and stone carvings a notable treat. Medievalists cherish the stately if warscarred castles and forts. And a surprisingly large contingent of World War II buffs descend on the islands' most recent relics—the best-preserved remnants of Hitler's entire "Atlantic Wall". Local devotees of these mostly monstrous concrete monuments believe they have as much right to adorn the sky-line as the fortifications of more remote eras.

Anyway, they would cost too much to demolish.

Where to Go

The family portrait of the Channel Islands looks like this: Jersey is the brash big brother, a bit raffish but very successful. Guernsey, the next in size, is calm, prudent and tasteful. Alderney is the country bumpkin, independent but generous. Sark and Herm are just fairytale characters, too small, in any event, to have any worries. All are uncommonly handsome and friendly.

Although they all belong to the same family, the islands insist on their individuality. First, they divide into two bailiwicks (units ruled by bailiffs): Jersey, plus some reefs near France; and the Bailiwick of Guernsey, encompassing all the rest. Each bailiwick has its own constitution and complex layers of government derived from ancient models.

Jersey and Alderney are on their own at the southern and northern extremities of the archipelago. Guernsey is more neighbourly: Herm and Sark are easy day excursions by boat. But none of the big three islands is more than 15 minutes from any other by air.

In this section the islands are considered in order of size, beginning with the biggest and liveliest of them all.   27

Jersey

Nature goes overboard to enhance Jersey's distinction as the southernmost of the British Isles. The Gulf Stream flows nearby, the prevailing winds are south-westerly, and the whole island tilts southward, to make the most of the long sunny days.

Thus spring comes earlier to Jersey. By March the early daffodils and anemones have gone to market in England; by May the rush begins for the new potatoes. Now called Jersey Royals, they are to ordinary spuds what a fresh *baguette*, the long, crisp French loaf, is to sliced supermarket bread.

Jersey's agricultural prosperity is often hidden behind hedges or high granite walls covered with lichen and wild flowers. Hidden, too, are most of the fine feudal manor houses. But you can't miss the graceful Jersey cows grazing in their fields. They are well looked after and, on a rainy day, you'll even see some of them clad in coats.

If the interior of the island specializes in discreet bucolic attractions, the coastline is a full-scale spectacular. There are about 20 miles of world-class beaches, and the rest of the coast tends to sensational cliffs.

The permanent population is 76,000. The catch is that the average Jersey family owns 1¼ cars. Add hire cars and all the ferry customers, and the traffic is strictly big-time.

Seeing St. Helier

Arriving in Jersey by sea, the traveller is unlikely to find the island's capital irresistible. The port of St. Helier, a big workaday installation, is not exactly glamorous. Inland, 15-storey apartment blocks and high-rise car-parks break the skyline. Still, there's a vaguely French quaintness about the town, part Brighton, part Breton.

St. Helier looks its best at high tide, when the ocean covers the rocky imperfections of the beaches, like fresh paint rejuvenating a house. Just watching the tide come in is a rare drama: it can rise by two inches per minute.

Guarding the harbour, as it has since Sir Walter Raleigh lived there as governor, **Elizabeth Castle** is a 12-minute walk from shore. But when the tide rises, the only practical way to get there or back is aboard an amphibious vehicle. Retired DUKW's ("ducks", colloquially) from World War II now earn their keep here as ferries.

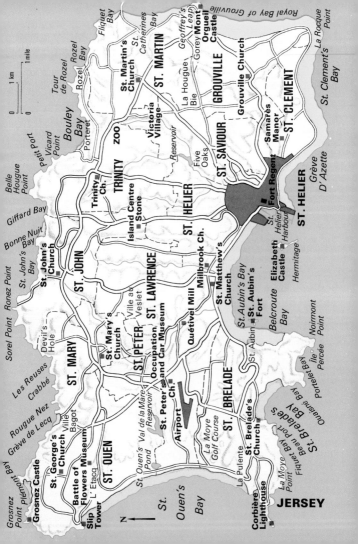

JERSEY

Queen Elizabeth I ordered the castle built to meet the challenge of new technology: the cannon. The weapons on view today range from a 17th-century 24-pounder to a jumbo 110-mm artillery piece from World War II. The occupying German forces added many cleverly camouflaged bunkers and towers for defence against attack by sea or air. The wide open space of the Lower Ward, like a town square, once contained a priory. But during the English Civil War in 1651, a mortar shell crashed through the roof and into the crypt which happened to be stocked with gunpowder. The blast ob-

literated the monastery and 40 people.

A breakwater built in 1872 links the castle with Hermitage Rock, where Jersey's patron saint lived and died. You can peer into the 12th-century **chapel** built around the natural stone bed which St. Helier slept on. The story of his murder, in the year 555, comes in various versions, but a sign in the parish church in town says he was killed "by an axe wielded by Saxon pirates". The last of Helier's miracles, the legend says, was to pick up his severed head, turn the other cheek, and walk away.

Towering over the harbour, the modern roof-line of **Fort Regent** looks like a white sun setting into a choppy sea. This is the latest design of a 19th-century bastion that never won any battle ribbons. Militarily, it was last used as a German barracks in World War II. Nowadays, it is the place to go in Jersey when it rains. The new Fort Regent is billed as one of Europe's most comprehensive entertainment, sports and conference centres. Under glass, locals and visitors share live shows, swimming pools, an "outdoor" café and several small **museums.** For local colour, visit the Museum of World Shells—a discriminating beachcomber's guide—and the Jersey Aquarium, featuring everything from angelfish to piranhas, with additional tanks down at toddlers' level. The

Tide's out, and visitors can walk all the way to Elizabeth Castle. **31**

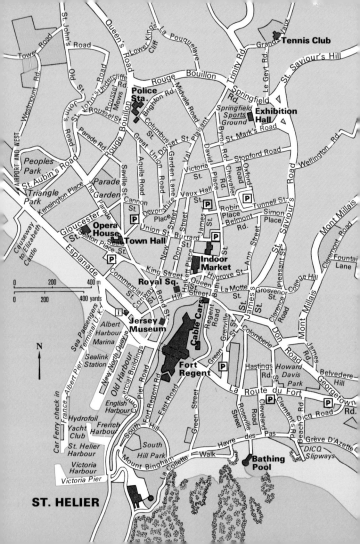

ST. HELIER

carousel, dodgems and fairground rides are free, once the basic admission fee has been paid, so children can have their fill of thrills. The old ramparts of Fort Regent still offer the best views in town.

In Pier Road, behind the island's bus terminus, the **Jersey Museum** occupies a distinguished Georgian house. Everything from ancient coins to modern golf trophies finds a place here. In the history section you can see a Bronze Age gold torque, a most elegant if hefty ornament weighing close to two pounds. Workmen excavating a basement in Lewis Street, near the seafront, dug up the 3,000-year-old bauble in 1888. From the 19th-century prison there is a punishment treadmill designed to keep a dozen prisoners hopping. One room of the museum is devoted to Lillie Langtry, the Jersey-born actress and socialite who scandalized Edwardian England. On display is an enormous gold-plated Smith & Wesson revolver, a gift from one of her admirers in Texas, Judge Roy Bean.

Until the beginning of the 18th century the **St. Helier Parish Church** was on the seafront. Reclamation work has pushed the Channel back about 300 yards. The Town Church, as it is known, has been expanded and rebuilt so many times over the last nine or ten centuries that its architectural pedigree is a bit hazy. The steeple is topless but the atmosphere within is most dignified. Like many Jersey churches, it has served for more than worship—as a meeting hall, a sanctuary for criminals, a warehouse and an arsenal.

The **Royal Square,** just to the east, has also witnessed more than its fair share of history. Prisoners used to be whipped and pilloried here, and witches burned, and the French lost a battle fought amongst its chestnut trees. The statue of King George II was erected by islanders grateful for a £300 royal subsidy for harbour works. It has been suggested that the statue was actually a leftover likeness of a Roman emperor, a bargain purchased from a passing Spanish sea-captain. But the rumour can't really be true: George is wearing the Order of the Garter. The square is surrounded by stately public buildings—the Royal Court House, the States Chamber (the island's parliament) and a bountifully stocked Public Library.

One public building that's always busy is the modern **Main Post Office** in Broad Street, 33

St. Helier's Victorian market is a cheerful, bountiful meeting place.

where tourists despatching postcards mingle with professional philatelists. British stamps were **34** used until 1969, when Jersey inaugurated its independent postal service. The post office has turned into a solid money-spinner. Thousands of collectors all over the world routinely buy sheets of each new Jersey stamp. And all those postcard writers add to the profits.

St. Helier's main shopping street, King Street, and several

are enough cheap watches in the shop windows to put Britain on Japan Standard Time.

Earthier shopping is concentrated in the **Central Market**, which was built in 1882. Under a high glass canopy, flowers, fruit and vegetables are displayed as if they were works of art. At the centre of all the hubbub, overweight goldfish swim in a pool surrounding a splendid fountain. Fish for dinner, however, are sold a few steps away in the **Beresford Market,** where you can buy anything from live lobster to fresh conger eel. Thanks to the influx of Portuguese workers, the market is also stocked with slabs of dried cod.

Escaping urban stress is easy in St. Helier: just head for the beaches or parks. One of the best, on the eastern edge of town, is **Howard Davis Park**. Its ten acres of shady trees, flower gardens and grass are beautifully tended. In a corner of the park the Union Jack flies side by side with the Stars and Stripes over a small cemetery for servicemen whose bodies were washed ashore in World War II. Brilliantly hued flowers cover the graves. The park was the gift of a local philanthropist, T.B. Davis, in memory of his son, Howard, killed in action in World War I.

of its offshoots have been turned into a **pedestrian precinct** providing sanctuary from the town's growling traffic. The familiar high street stores are there, plus local specialists appealing to the tourist temperament with VAT-free, low-duty perfumes, jewellery, cameras, alcohol and tobacco. There

Round the Island

Westward from St. Helier sprawls the inviting sandy crescent of **St. Aubin's Bay,** shallow enough for children's pursuits and ideal for windsurfing and water-skiing. The Jekyll and Hyde character of the sea is magnified on Jersey beaches. In the afternoon you may have to plod a couple of hundred yards down the gentle slope to dip a toe in the Channel; in the evening the tide roars in, flooding the lot.

Halfway round the bay, just inland from the coast road, the 19th-century St. Matthew's Church at Millbrook is famous as the **Glass Church.** In 1934

the French artist René Lalique was commissioned to create the windows, screens, font and cross, all in original designs. To startling effect, he used colourless glass. The small church has become such a popular tourist attraction that a three-minute recorded commentary drones forth every few minutes.

On the west side of the bay, **St. Aubin** is a friendly fishing village jammed between the harbour and a hill. It is the head-

Innocent waves lap deadly rocks, marked by historic Corbière light.

In the pink: Jersey's carnations are flown to the English market.

quarters of the Royal Channel Islands Yacht Club. Commercial fishing boats, dinghies and yachts are moored in front of attractive old houses from which you expect grizzled fishing captains to emerge at any moment. Like St. Helier, visible across the bay, St. Aubin has its own offshore fort, begun in the 16th century. You can walk there over a causeway at low tide, but don't get caught out.

Noirmont Point, the windy western extremity of St. Aubin's Bay, is an obvious strategic strongpoint bristling with German defensive positions from World War II. Looming above the Maginot-style bunkers is a four-storey concrete tower designed as the eyes and brains of a network of coastal artillery batteries. Three of these streamlined towers still stand on heights around the Jersey coast—the only such relics along what was Hitler's Atlantic Wall.

Continuing clockwise around the coast, **Portelet Bay** looks like a perfect little port for a storm, and the bathing is good. The tiny island in the middle of the bay has a melancholy story to tell. In 1721 a local sea captain, Philippe Janvrin, died of the plague aboard his ship. The authorities barred the coffin from Jersey. So widow and mourners attended a funeral service ashore, watching as the captain was buried on his own little isle.

Ouaisné Bay, a suntrap of a

beach in the afternoon, is the site of La Cotte de St. Brelade, a leading Stone Age lair. Since its discovery in 1881 the cave has been picked over by generations of archaeologists, who have found hundreds of thousands of Palaeolithic souvenirs. When Prince Charles was a student at Cambridge he tried his hand at the "dig". The cave is closed to the public.

Hotels, cafés and souvenir stands line the sweeping sands of **St. Brelade's Bay**, but the Germans provided the sea wall, now a promenade, as an anti-tank barrier. The bay here is popular for swimming, wind-surfing and water-skiing. Just **39** above the western edge of the beach, the **Parish Church of St. Brelade** may have been founded by the Irish voyager, St. Brendan. Until the middle of the last century smoking was permitted in a gallery upstairs, and many a pipe was puffed to punctuate the sermon. The early Norman **Fishermen's Chapel**, nearby, may be the oldest Christian temple on the island. It's just above the beach, so a fisherman in a hurry could have clambered from his prayers to his boat in a matter of seconds.

At **Corbière Point,** Jersey's southwestern extremity, one of those 1940's artillery coordinating towers has been adapted for peacetime service. Crowned by an airport-style observation deck, it controls sea traffic as "Jersey Radio". The rocky promontory below the tower has been one of the more popular places for shipwrecks over the centuries. The gulls soar and shriek above the rugged grandeur of this coast, as if waiting for developments. In 1873 the first concrete lighthouse in the British Isles was built here. It now runs on automatic pilot. In a storm the ocean spray sometimes goes over the top of the Corbière Lighthouse—136 feet above high tide!

St. Ouen's Bay has a beach big, broad and beautiful enough to grace any island twice Jersey's size. The open sea rolls ashore here, and surfers turn out in their hundreds to take advantage of championship conditions. But the tide is so rough that only expert swimmers are advised to challenge it. Covering almost the entire west coast, the beach measures 4 miles from end to sandy end. That means room enough for sunbathers and racing fans, too: motorcycles and racing cars regularly use a stretch of the beach as their track.

During Napoleon's time, the British built nine defensive towers along St. Ouen's Bay. The occupying Germans also realized that this golden beach was an ideal target for an invasion fleet, so they booby-trapped the beach and built a long re-inforced anti-tank wall. This remains a useful defence against exaggerated tides. Behind the sea-wall are dunes, marshes and a nature reserve around **St. Ouen's Pond**, where the most exotic migrant birds join the resident ducks and geese.

At **L'Etacq,** just inland from the north end of the beach, a handicrafts centre claims to be the only place in the world producing walking sticks from cabbages. Jersey Giant Cabbages grow taller than a man. The leaves are almost inedible, but the stalk, when dried and painted, is strong and long enough to serve as a cane, with the off cuts used to make shoehorns, fly-swatters and other souvenirs. In case you want to grow your own walking sticks, they also sell cabbage seeds.

Grosnez Point, at the northwest corner of the island, summarizes Jersey at its most spectacular: awesome cliffs, the remains of what is probably a 14th-century castle, and the sea spray salting the aroma of heather and gorse. From here, on a perfect day, you can see Guernsey and Sark, and as far beyond as Alderney. Only a gloomy hint of **Grosnez Castle** still stands: a main gateway, bastions and a narrow moat. It's thought to have been a refuge in the Middle Ages for islanders fleeing the lowlands at times of French invasion.

The whole northern coast consists of dramatic, flower-topped cliffs, easily explorable along well-marked paths. Here and there the granite walls embrace an intimate bay. **Plémont Bay,** for instance, is sandy and well shielded but the sea can be dangerous. At low tide you can walk to caves that were inhabited in the Stone Age.

Protective cliffs and hills spare the beach at **Grève de Lecq** from all but the north wind. Since the earliest times it has appealed to potential invaders as a roomy landing zone. The defenders' reaction was to build a rash of fortifications, from the Iron Age to World War II, giving the hills considerable historic interest. The National Trust for Jersey has restored a group of barracks from the Napoleonic Wars, and, up the hill, an 18th-century fort and gun battery. Nearby earthworks may be more than 2,000 years old.

A mile east of Grève de Lecq, the ocean's fury reaches a climax at **Devil's Hole.** A footpath leads out onto a high peninsula beyond the breakers for, among other sights, a head-on view of cliffs under siege. And you look down at the blow-hole through which the sea concentrates its rage in explosive spasms. (Check the tide table in the local newspaper before you go, or you may see nothing more than the meekest lapping waves.)

The charmingly named **Bonne Nuit Bay** (Good Night) has a small beach and harbour. Less than a mile to the east is Jersey's highest point, all of 485 feet above sea level. Radio transmitting towers are planted **41**

here to take advantage of the altitude; don't be alarmed if your car radio squawks in protest. Continuing clockwise, lush greenery descends to the edge of **Bouley Bay,** with a steep pebble beach, from which scuba divers and anglers share the clear seas. A fishing hamlet and 19th century barracks (now a hotel and restaurant) determine the mood at **Rozel Bay,** the last of the north coast beaches, considered ideal for children.

From the heights above the north-east coast you may be able to see Les Ecréhous, windswept islands belonging to Jersey. On these rocky islets stand an ancient chapel's ruins and several houses, used by occasional fishermen or escapist holidaymakers. Jersey's other "offshore" possessions are the similarly bleak Minquiers (known familiarly as the Monkeys), about halfway between St. Helier and St. Malo, France.

Rounding the north-east corner of the island, **Fliquet Bay,** a small sandy strand, offers the first glimpse of the notorious **St. Catherine's Breakwater.** This grotesquely oversized pier, nearly half a mile long, dates from the 1840's. The British Admiralty, alarmed at French intentions, decided to make **St. Catherine's Bay** a port fit for an armada. The project was abandoned as an expensive blunder. Nowadays, the great stone arm thrusting into the sea brings pleasure to strollers and anglers, and calms the waves for bathers.

At the south end of St. Catherine's Bay, **Geoffrey's Leap** is a cliff to brood over, not jump over. According to local legend, a felon named Geoffrey was sentenced to be executed here. The technique was to toss the condemned man over the side and onto the sharp rocks below. Rather miraculously, he fell into unscheduled waves, survived, and returned to the clifftop to claim his freedom. A bit of a show-off, Geoffrey couldn't resist leaping again. But this time the tide had fled and he plunged to his fate on the rocks.

The village of **Gorey** makes a pretty picture: a row of low white houses around a mostly-for-pleasure port, all in the shadow of Jersey's oldest castle. **Mont Orgueil Castle** has everything: history, a certain

Jersey giant cabbages taste horrid but make unusual walking sticks. Overleaf: coast near Devil's Hole.

charm, and beautiful vistas. Its French name means Mount Pride, and justly so, for this rugged fortress resisted many full-scale attacks by French raiding parties from the 13th to 15th centuries. The invention of the cannon, though, shattered its invulnerability. Still, it has served as a strong point as recently as 1945, when the Germans manned anti-aircraft and machine guns on Mont Orgueil's heights.

From the ticket office at the castle entrance, itself high above the harbour, it's a climb up 198 steps to the top of this conglomerate of walls, halls, wards, towers and bastions. Along the way, there are several lush little lawns and gardens with benches for those inclined to take things at a leisurely pace. The view from the summit reveals miles of desirable beaches up and down Jersey's east coast, and Normandy can be seen in the distance.

A small wax museum dramatizes incidents from the castle's history, with recorded explanations in French and English. And there's a museum of medieval weapons, neolithic tools and other artefacts discovered on the site.

Artefacts of modern manufacture attract coach loads of tourists to the **Jersey Pottery** in Gorey. Several acres of gardens and a highly rated restaurant add to the interest. Visitors wander through the airy, cheerful factory watching the mould-makers, clay-throwers and artists at work. But plugged into transistors or chatting with workmates, the artisans are oblivious to the audience. The firm's pots, plates, wall-clocks, lamps and candlesticks are on sale under the same roof.

The beach stretching south from Gorey goes by the smartest name of all: the **Royal Bay of Grouville.** Queen Victoria herself bestowed the title. The coastline here, rich in 18th and 19th century fortifications, attracts crowds of wading birds, such as the oystercatcher with its bright orange bill. In the 1940's the Germans chose Grouville as the source of sand for the concrete of their gigantic military construction programme. The loss of a million tons of sand lowered the beach level considerably, but not enough to deter postwar throngs of sunbathers and swimmers.

Pots arise before your eyes as the wheel turns at the Jersey Pottery, a landmark on the tourist track.

La Rocque Harbour, just to the south, is a lazy little port with a soft white sand beach. This is where a French invasion succeeded in 1781. Flagrantly disregarding the norms of sportsmanship, the French timed the landing for a night when the Jersey militia was off celebrating a holiday.

St. Clement's Bay, facing south, is sandy and rocky, and at low tide the beachcombers fan out over the rock pools and gullies. The most impressive building in St. Clement's parish is **Samarès Manor,** a patrician house in the best of architectural taste. It is surrounded by delightful gardens, which are open to the public (admission is charged). In feudal times only the lords of manors were allowed to keep pigeons, and here you can see an authentic *colombier* or dovecot, a big round apartment block for pigeons.

Every one of Jersey's 12 parishes has some coastline, even if it requires a bit of fiddling. Access to the sea was considered vital in the earliest times, not least as an escape route. Under Norman law a fugitive could claim asylum in any parish church, gaining free passage from there to the sea and exile. St. Saviour parish, essentially an inland domain, scrapes through with a slipway at **Le Dicq,** on the border of St. Helier. By coincidence, a massive rock on the beach, alongside the slipway, was a favourite spot for the exiled author, Victor Hugo. He used to clamber to the top, sit down and seek inspiration in the sight and sound of the waves.

St. Saviour Parish Church is more widely known for its human interest than its 12th-century architecture. The rector, the Rev. Dean William Le Breton, was the father of Lillie Langtry, one of the 19th century's most glamorous "women of the world". She first rocked British society when it became known that she was the mistress of the Prince of Wales. She later had a daughter by the prince's nephew, Prince Louis of Battenberg. Eventually she settled down as a Lady: marrying a baronet, she became Lady de Bathe.

As an actress Lillie Langtry was most praised for her Rosalind in Shakespeare's *As You Like It*. But her fame, in Britain and the United States (which she toured in her own train), was based more on her perfect profile and eventful private life than on her acting talent. The "Jersey Lily" died in Monte Carlo in 1929. She is buried in the parish churchyard.

Inland Sights

After hectic St. Helier and a round of beaches, we turn to Jersey's thoroughly charming interior. Here is a land of narrow country roads bordered by flowered granite walls or tall hedges and ivy-clad trees. Here, too, are calm, green, enticing valleys, perhaps barely wider than a railway viaduct. It is a sun-blessed sanctuary for farmers and tax-shy millionaires. Aside from the natural beauties, there are tourist attractions for many tastes. All those covered here charge admission. We approach them roughly from west to east.

Battle of Flowers Museum, St. Ouen. The life work of Miss Florence Bechelet, who invented her own art form. With an acute eye for accuracy and infinite patience, she has constructed scores of floats to compete in Battle of Flowers parades since 1934. Using dyed thistles, straw and flowers, she spends up to 1,400 hours confecting each float. The most remarkable of her prize-winners are displayed.

St. Peter's Bunker, St. Peter's Village. This six-room underground bunker, built by forced labour in 1942, is one of the best preserved and documented "monuments" to the German occupation. It is crammed with exhibits as various as an original Enigma decoding machine, a blanket beater used on Russian prisoners and a pin-up picture of Hermann Göring. Sound effects are provided by the Horst Wessel song and a sample of Hitler's ranting. Indications of life on the Jersey home front include propaganda newspapers and occupation money, homemade shoes, and letters from informers to the Gestapo.

Jersey Motor Museum, a few steps away from the bunker, has military overtones, as well. Among the exhibits are British, American and German army vehicles, including the two-and-a-half-ton Rolls Royce Phantom III used by Field Marshal Montgomery during the run-up to D-Day. On a more modest scale, there is a Model T Ford from 1926, "the original Lizzie", which cost £120 when new, as well as motorcycles and motorized children's cars.

Strawberry Farm, St. Peter. Twenty acres of strawberry fields surround a motley collection of tourist attractions: a miniature village, craftsmen's workshops, a café and a refurbished World War II bunker. A big and relatively luxurious underground command centre is now equipped with swastika 49

It's always feeding time for the fascinating specimens in the hothouse at Jersey Butterfly Centre.

flags, uniforms, radio and telephone equipment. When you come up for air they'll sell you a strawberry trifle, or strawberries topped with Jersey cream that stands up like a meringue.

La Mare Vineyards, St. Mary. A working vineyard is such a novelty in the Channel Islands that they let the tourists in to watch the grapes growing. The Clos de la Mare white wine is very fruity and appetizing; the Clos de Seyval is slightly sweet. This family-run establishment also produces cider, a local tradition since Norman days.

Jersey Butterfly Centre, St. Mary. Here you can enter a hot, muggy greenhouse and mingle with some beautiful creatures: butterflies from

Asia, South America and Europe fluttering close enough to touch. As butterflies require a diet of tasty flowers and leaves, the place is laid out as a rich tropical garden. (Serious lepidopterists will also want to look for migrating butterflies and moths on the loose all over the island, especially in summer and autumn.)

Le Moulin de Quétivel, St. Peter's Valley. Probably 800 years old and newly restored to working condition, this water-mill shows every step in the traditional process of grinding grain.

German Military Underground Hospital, St. Peter's Valley. This was the most elaborate of the World War II projects in the Channel Islands—an underground city so big that even claustrophobic visitors are scarcely bothered. It was a wonder of sophisticated equipment, from air-conditioning to a telephone exchange. Slave workers and civilian prisoners controlled by the paramilitary Organisation Todt excavated 14,000 tons of rock to create a grid of tunnels big enough to drive tanks through. The forested hill above the hospital entrance is man-made, consisting of the excavated earth and stone from the tunnels below. The installa-tion was originally designed as artillery barracks and work-shops but became a hospital in 1944. The brightly lit, white-washed tunnels contain hospi-tal and military equipment as well as pertinent maps and documents; a video production summarizes the war's effect on the islanders. At the end of the tour, an underground souvenir shop sells, among other novel-ties, miniature guns, book-matches reproducing *Achtung Minen!* warnings, and "real bullet" key rings.

Jersey Zoo, Trinity. For-mally, the establishment is called the Jersey Wildlife Pre-servation Trust, and its aim is to save threatened species of animals from extinction. This is all very earnest, but the famous Jersey Zoo is still a lot of fun for any tourist, and an out-standing educational attraction for children. You'd have to be heartless not to love the baby gorilla as he devises new mis-chief, or be fascinated by the orang-utan trailing his fur coat like an anxious Hollywood producer. There are inhabitants as beautiful as the golden lion tamarin and the snow leopard, as comical as the ruffed lemur and the spectacled bear, and as frankly unappealing as the rhi-noceros iguana. What they all have in common is their rarity **51**

and the need to save them from the fate of the Dodo bird (the zoo's ironic trademark). From its headquarters in an 18th-century manor house in the middle of 20 landscaped acres, the Trust is a world leader in breeding exotic animals in captivity and promoting wildlife conservation overseas. Among the many successes is the Mauritius pink pigeon, formerly on the verge of extinction; newly bred birds have been sent back to the Indian Ocean island, which was also the Dodo's home. The zoo was founded in 1959 by author and zoologist Gerald Durrell, whose books and television programmes keep Jersey in the limelight for nature lovers everywhere.

The Orchid Trust, Victoria Village, Trinity. This is one of the most comprehensive orchid collections open to the public. There are five tropical houses and a landscaped display area.

La Hougue Bie, Grouville. This archaeological site is one of Europe's finest Neolithic tombs, dating back to about 2000 B.C. Similar in design to megalithic monuments in England, Ireland and nearby Brittany, this passage grave is 33 feet long, roofed and walled with giant stone slabs. La Hougue Bie may have been the mausoleum of a local Neolithic dynasty. Looters—probably Viking raiders in the 10th century—got here first, but you can explore the empty four-foot high tomb. La Hougue Bie is covered by a 40-foot mound of earth, stone and shells, now a cheerful grassy hill. A medieval chapel and a 16th-century one stand atop the hill, presumably built to impose Christian dominance over the pagan site.

La Société Jersiaise, which studies all aspects of the island's heritage, owns and manages La Hougue Bie. In addition to a railway exhibition, there are three museums on the site: an archaeological collection going back to Neanderthal days; an agricultural museum featuring old-time Jersey farm implements; and a military occupation museum. It's hard to avoid World War II relics anywhere in the Channel Islands, so it may have been inevitable that the Germans would build a large communications bunker almost next door to the Stone Age passage grave. Inside the bunker are displayed propaganda leaflets, weapons, radio equipment and the menu for the last supper the German troops ate before the surrender: 85 grammes of wurst, bread, butter and coffee.

Cattle Country

How now, brown cow? Handsome is the answer, with patches of white on their tan coats, and intelligent faces with big eyes. Gentle, too, because (the legend says) Jersey cows were always tended by women, the men being away fishing or warring.

Other countries put monarchs, civic leaders or heroes on their banknotes, but Jersey has other priorities. Hold up to the light a Jersey £1 note and look: the watermark immortalizes the portrait of a Jersey cow.

The only competition in producing the world's richest milk comes from the Guernsey cow, which accounts for marginally more golden cream. Both islands are fiercely protective of their breeds. Imports of milk-cows have been forbidden in Jersey since 1789, in Guernsey since 1819.

Jersey's bizarre Long Jack cabbage, which grows on stalks taller than a man, was originally planted on the island as a supplemental feed for cattle. The leaves, though not quite fit for human consumption, filled out the cows' winter diet; the stalks turned out to be ideal for use as walking-sticks.

53

Guernsey

All the resident bankers, retired millionaires and high-tech horticulturalists add to Guernsey's air of dignity. Yet the island is anything but stodgy. Where else could you find a tomato museum, a chapel built of seashells and broken china, a marina in a quarry, and World War II bunkers ambushing the tourists with hamburgers and ice cream?

The westernmost of the Channel Islands, Guernsey is vulnerable to Atlantic gales—as a local museum of shipwrecks illustrates. But the problem is quite remote for summer holiday-makers, who can always find a sheltered bay if the fresh air does more than ruffle the hair and gladden the lungs.

With an area of less than 25 square miles, the island is small enough to get to know in a fortnight. If you should get lost among the greenhouses and dairy farms, in narrow country roads screened by high walls, the best advice is to keep going until you see the sea.

On the map, Guernsey looks like a right-angled triangle facing left. Cliffs and coves comprise the south coast; the northwest (the hypotenuse) has sandy beaches to spare; and on the east side is St. Peter Port,

the island's capital and major port.

The island is inhabited by 53,000 people and 2,300 cows. Guernseys, of course.

St. Peter Port

Here at last is an island port that looks the part and warms the heart of the arriving sailor, fisherman or seaborne tourist. A castle, close on 800 years old, shields a dynamic harbour lined with steep-roofed granite houses standing shoulder-to-shoulder. Behind them, a stately town on a hillside culminates in a bristle of church steeples above grand old trees.

A 17th-century report raved about the harbour, "able to contain the greatest Navy that ever sailed upon the Ocean, fenced from the fury of the winds..." The scene today is a lively pageant of ferries and freighters, hydrofoils and sailboats; every year 10,000 yachts come to call. The outer port is dredged for access at all tides.

Close to the seaside promenade, though, the notorious low tide puts many boats into involuntary dry dock twice a day. Some boat owners take advantage of this to paint the hull or do repairs while the sea is out of town.

Until the Victorians built the southern harbour wall, **Castle Cornet** was on its own island.

At day's end, yachts and a visiting gull settle down in St. Peter Port.

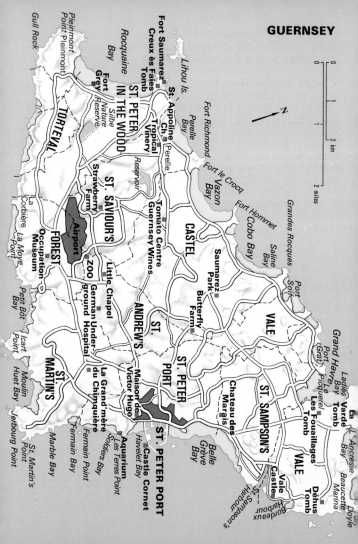

GUERNSEY

0 1 2 km
0 1 2 miles

N

Gull Rock

Pleinmont Point Pleinmont

Fort Saumarez
Creux ès Faies Tomb
Fort Grey

Rocquaine Bay

ST. PETER IN THE WOOD

St. Appoline Ch.
Tropical Vinery

Lihou Is.

Perelle Bay

Perelle

Fort Richmond

Fort le Crocq

Vazon Bay

Fort Hommet

Cobo Bay

Grandes Rocques

Saline Bay

Port Soif

Silbe Nature Reserve

Reservoir

Tomato Centre
Guernsey Wines

CASTEL

Saumarez Park

Butterfly Farm

VALE

La Corbière
La Moye Point

Strawberry Farm

ST. SAVIOUR'S

FOREST

Occupation Museum

Airport

ZOO

Little Chapel

German Underground Hospital

ANDREW'S

ST. ANDREW'S

La Grand'mère du Chimquière

Maison de Victor Hugo

ST. PETER

ST. PORT

Chateau des Marais

ST. SAMPSON'S

La Vardé
Grand Havre Bay
Port Grat
Port Picquerel
Les Fouaillages Tomb

VALE

L'Ancresse Bay
Beaucette Marina

Déhus Tomb

Vale Castle

Petit Bôt Bay

ST. MARTIN'S

La Grand'mère du Chimquière

Les Terres Point

Soldier's Bay

Belle Grève Bay

ST. PETER PORT

Castle Cornet

Havelet Bay

Aquarium

Bordeaux Harbour

St. Sampson's Harbour

St. Peter Port Harbour

Icart Point
Moulin Huet Bay
St. Martin's Point
Marble Bay
Fermain Bay
Fermain Point
Jerbourg Point

In the English Civil War the Royalists were able to hold out there for nine years against the Parliamentary forces in the town. It has been a low-profile fort since 1672, when lightning touched off the ammunition stores, bringing down the towering central keep. But many of the other elements of medieval military architecture are there, from the barbican to the citadel, plus World War II accretions as part of Hitler's Atlantic Wall programme.

Inside the castle walls, too, are compact **museums** specializing in the maritime and military history of Guernsey and the island's experiences of

St. Peter Port's High Street begins at the venerable Parish Church.

World War II occupation. And you'll find a refreshing garden begun by a Very Important Prisoner, General John Lambert, Cromwell's deputy, incarcerated from 1660–70 for political crimes. Here he grew the Guernsey Lily, which became the island's official flower.

If you take pictures, try to arrive at the castle's Royal Battery ahead of time for the Midday Gun. Re-enacting an old ceremony, two redcoats fire **57** an artillery salute to St. Peter Port. The uniforms, the gun smoke and the background of the port make a dramatic snapshot—marred only, perhaps, by camera shake as you jump at the gun's roar.

The most majestic church in Guernsey, and probably in all the Channel Islands, is the **Parish Church** of St. Peter Port. Familiarly known as the Town Church, its sturdy steeple rises above the waterfront townscape. First mentioned in a document of 1048, it has served many religious and civic purposes. The inside walls are heavy with memorial tablets recounting the bravery of local warriors. Among the most notable is Sir Isaac Brock, whose victory near Niagara in 1812 saved Canada from annexation by the United States. A stained-glass window portraying St. Peter replaces one "destroyed by war action" in 1944. The window was actually shattered, not by the Ger-

Fisherman's oilskins foil the breeze on Castle Pier; skylights invite the sunshine into Guernsey's classic early 19th-century market halls.

Dress is casual at ferry port but traditional in bric-a-brac market.

mans, but by an exceptionally powerful American air force bomb, intended for a suspected German submarine in the harbour.

Until the middle of the 18th century the church was all but surrounded by street markets. Then, for the sake of decorum, the merchants were moved up the hill. A tourist guidebook published in 1838 called the new, hygienic fish market one of the finest in Europe. The **Markets** are still a tourist at-traction for their combination of historic architecture and brisk activity. The best local produce, artfully displayed, competes with imports like Swiss cheeses, German sausages and French bread flown in from Cherbourg. On Thursday afternoons in Market Square costumed vendors sell souvenirs and handicrafts from candy-striped stalls.

For all kinds of shopping, the cobbled High Street and adjacent traffic-free streets are lined with modern shops vaunting the advantages of VAT-free prices. The **General Post Office** in Smith Street sells stamps and philatelic material **61** among displays of museum-worthy postal relics. The Bailiwick of Guernsey, like Jersey, is an independent postal and monetary power. A Guernseyman, Thomas de la Rue (1793–1866), founded the great British printing company bearing his name, which issues stamps and banknotes on behalf of many countries.

Writer in Residence

The French novelist, poet and political activist Victor Hugo (1802–1885) was granted Guernsey citizenship, but he never learned to speak English. "When England wants to chat with me," he used to say, "let her learn my language." His heart always belonged to France, which he could see from his topfloor study in Hauteville House. As he told fellow exiles, "The tear in our eyes is called France".

Hugo's exile, imposed by Napoleon III, began in Jersey, but he was tossed out after three years for publishing a letter critical of Queen Victoria. Guernsey welcomed him and he returned the affection. His book, *Les Travailleurs de la Mer* (Toilers of the Sea), is dedicated to "the rock of hospitality and freedom ... the island of Guernsey, severe and gentle".

The **Royal Court House** in Rue du Manoir dates from 1799. In the main courtroom the Guernsey parliament, the Assembly of the States, holds its debates, in English nowadays. From the gallery above, the public can watch proceedings, which are attended by the non-voting Lieutenant-Governor and presided over by the Bailiff in his robes of office.

Candie Gardens, a relatively small but extravagant park, exploits a priceless view over the port and the English Channel. Before they went public, about a century ago, the gardens were the front lawn of Candie House, now the Priaulx Library. The library holds a remarkable collection of over 30,000 books and manuscripts, documenting Guernsey's history since the 15th century.

The new **Guernsey Museum and Art Gallery,** in Candie Gardens, is designed as a cluster of octagons, inspired by a Victorian bandstand now incorporated in the building. This is the place to go for a quick briefing on the island and its people, with exhibits ranging from chunks of the island's granite foundation to ship models and archaic farm tools. The art gallery is used for temporary exhibitions, usually by local artists.

Hugo braves the wind from France in Guernsey's Candie Gardens.

North of Candie Gardens, still high above the port, the **Beau Séjour Leisure Centre** is the modern core of community activities. These include rock concerts, roller skating, swimming, squash and softball (the American sport seems to have captivated Guernsey). Though much less ambitious than Jersey's Fort Regent complex, Beau Séjour is a good bet for a rainy day. If the weather's really that bad, they have a sun-lamp "solarium" to overcome your pallor.

There's a little bit of Paris in St. Peter Port: the big white **Hauteville House,** owned by the city of Paris. Victor Hugo and his wife lived in it throughout his 15 years of exile in Guernsey; he installed his mistress a few streets away in a house he could signal to from his bedroom. This is where he wrote his classic novel *Les Misérables,* at the rate of 20 pages every morning. During visiting hours the mansion is often packed with French pilgrims, milling about in Hugo's bizarre writing-and-pacing lookout and other unusual rooms. The author was an accomplished carpenter and an adventurous interior decorator.

63

Round the Coast

On the southern outskirts of St. Peter Port, just beyond the bathing pool, the **Aquarium** is tucked away in the remains of an old tunnel. It's both enterprising and educational; among the innovations are one-way mirrors for spying on shy fish. Many of the specimens were donated by local fishermen, but the collection also includes some tropical species.

A winding road climbs through a forest to Fort George, now a fashionable suburban housing estate. Until June, 1944, Fort George really was a fort (built toward the end of the 18th century), but Allied bombers flattened it to hamper German preparations for Europe's D-Day.

You can walk, drive or take a ferry from St. Peter Port south

At Cobo Bay, sunbathers watch the children play a sort of croquet.

to **Fermain Bay,** a pretty beach of smooth stones, isolated in green surroundings. High above the bay stands a curious white landmark which the locals call the Pepper Pot. It's a guardhouse big enough for only one soldier.

The 6 miles of south coast —an undulating cliff wall— begins at **Jerbourg Point,** a cape with views of rocks and reefs and, on a clear day, Jersey. Cliff paths slice through wild shrubs and flowers hum-

ming with bees, butterflies and birds. **Icart Point, La Moye Point** and **La Corbière** may not be the highest capes you'll ever see, but, as the sea crashes onto the rocks below, they have a spectacular beauty of their own.

Sheltered in cliff folds are several desirable beaches, once fishermen's ports: **Petit Port, Moulin Huet, Petit Bôt** and

Trinity House

Almost everywhere else in the world, lighthouses are owned and operated by governments. But in England, Wales and the Channel Islands the responsibility rests with Trinity House, a 700-year-old charity for seafarers. The Trinity House Brethren built their first lighthouse in 1680, in the Isles of Scilly. They now operate some 90 lighthouses, 30 lightships and hundreds of lighted buoys.

Construction of Guernsey's Hanois Reef beacon, 117 feet tall, was begun in 1860. The keepers and their families live in carefully gardened Trinity House cottages overlooking Portelet Harbour. Two crews of three men carry out alternate tours of duty on the rock light. When the sea is rough they are provisioned, and change shifts, by helicopter.

Portelet. You may have to clamber down difficult paths to reach them.

The westernmost cliffs of **Pleinmont Point** are the culmination of all this. They form a glorious Atlantic headland, wild but for television towers and one of those streamlined concrete forts from World War II. More than a mile offshore, the Hanois Lighthouse announces a particularly dreadful reef and the dangers in general of this part of the coast. The light has been faithfully flashing since 1862.

Rocquaine Bay, the first on the sandy west coast, is more than a mile long, with alternating rocky outcrops and beaches. Atop a small rocky peninsula here stands **Fort Grey,** an early 18th-century coastal tower. Locally it has long been known as the "cup and saucer", because of its white tower set upon a wide granite base. The landmark now serves as the **Fort Grey Maritime Museum.** Its maps, pictures and exhibits contain profound revelations about the dangerous waters hereabouts, and the archaeologists who dive for wrecks. A cannon from the Royal Navy frigate *Boreas,* lost on the Hanois reef in 1807 and recovered after 163 years on the bottom, now aims through the

fort's outer wall at the reefs where she met her doom.

The next fort to the northwest, **Fort Saumarez,** is a strange feat of World War II improvisation: a four-storey observation tower tacked onto an 18th-century Martello-style tower. It's a nice fit, if not aesthetically suitable. Nearby, in excellent repair, is a prehistoric passage grave called **Le Creux ès Faies** (Fairies' Grotto). The Germans built a bunker next to it but did not disturb the empty tomb.

Lihou Island, under the surveillance of Fort Saumarez, is linked to the headland of l'Erée by a centuries-old causeway.

Guernsey's are yellow: phone box in classic form on Rocquaine Bay.

You can walk out to the island twice a day at low tide, but make sure to check on what time you should return. A friendly family owns the 18-acre island and its big modern farmhouse. The livestock consists of a docile white horse, an affectionate donkey, throngs of rabbits, and assorted geese, peacocks and chickens. The ruins of an ancient Benedictine priory have survived centuries of vicissitudes. Visitors can buy souvenir postcards, home-made jams and biscuits on the island, but no postage stamps. From 1966 to 1969 Lihou took itself so seriously that it issued its own stamps.

Perelle Bay, the next inlet northward, is mostly rocky but, in consequence, never crowded. Just inland, the **Chapel of St. Apolline** is a faithfully restored little 14th-century church dedicated to the patron saint of dentists. Faint but fascinating ancient frescoes may be seen on the inner walls.

Vazon Bay is a whopper of a beach, a delicious prospect for sunbather, swimmer or surfer. This was the unlikely setting for a shipwreck in 1937. When the

Stitches in Time

Channel Islanders have been busy knitting since perhaps the 15th century. Queen Elizabeth I favoured Guernsey stockings; Mary Queen of Scots wore a pair to her execution. They sold like hot cakes in England and France under suggestive names such as Amorous Desire and Mortal Sin. Jersey sweaters became known thanks to the number of Jersey men who entered the Newfoundland enterprises at the beginning of the 17th century, giving rise to local shipbuilding and consequently the supply of jerseys for the mariners.

Guernseys are traditionally knitted from thick navy blue wool, whereas jerseys are thinner and come in various colours. Guernseys have no side seams, as they are worked in rounds on eleven or nine small needles (nowadays a circular needle is often used). Jerseys usually have an all-over pattern; guernseys are more plain, with a pattern knitted into the shoulder straps.

The Island fishermen have been wearing similar spray-resistant woollen garments for centuries. But a stained glass window in one parish church may be exaggerating with its portrait of St. Peter himself wearing a guernsey.

SS Briseis sank in calm seas, the crew easily reached shore ... and so did much of the freighter's cargo: barrels of wine. The locals pitched into the salvage operation with such enthusiasm that, according to a contemporary account, "amazing scenes of drunkenness" ensued on the beach.

Fort Hommet, an amalgam of 19th-century British and 20th-century German military architecture, has been partly restored, so you can explore it. The view from the top is a winning panorama of Vazon Bay. Most of the World War II bunkers around the island are now covered with grass, making them appear almost innocuous ... as their original camouflage efforts intended. Some German forts have been transformed into cafés or public conveniences.

Continuing clockwise, two roomy beaches, **Cobo Bay** and **Saline Bay,** are popular with sunbathers, swimmers and surfers. The next along the way is **Port Soif,** a small, almost circular bay surrounded by big, climbable rocks. The last of the west coast bays, **Grand Havre,** contains a fine suntanning beach known as **Ladies Bay.** All the beaches change character according to the state of the sea, being best for rockpooling at low tide, and for swimming at the high.

Just inland, Guernsey's 18-hole golf course stretches over scenic but difficult terrain. The sea views are magnificent, but the golfers have to avoid obstacles such as prehistoric monuments and World War II pillboxes. In addition, Guernsey cattle graze between the fairways.

Alongside the 5th hole, the well signposted ancient monument called **Les Fouaillages** may be older than the Pyramids of Egypt. Stones form a triangle 20 yards at its longest, perhaps patterned after an axehead or a flint ... or could it have been the map of Guernsey? Inside the tomb archaeologists found chunks of decorated pottery more than 6,000 years old. In the late Stone Age an additional monument was built atop the original passage grave.

Two mounds rise above the golfers' 17th green: a German bunker and **La Varde**, a 40-foot-long passage grave, the largest on the island. You have to bend low to enter, but in the centre of the tomb a six-footer can safely stand tall and examine the huge capstones.

L'Ancresse Common is a green belt along the north coast, shared by golfers, ramblers, cows and goats. It overlooks the virtually flawless beach of **L'Ancresse Bay**. At low tide you might run out of steam, pursuing the sea hundreds of yards down the slope of sand. This beach, so wide and accessible, must have been an invader's dream since time immemorial. Hence the defenders planted Martello towers every few hundred yards, followed by the World War II anti-tank wall that now serves as a breakwater. What are loosely called Martello towers in Guernsey were actually built before the first "real" Martello was devised in Corsica around 1790. The two-storey cylindrical design, though, is similar—nothing fancy, as though modelled on the sandcastles produced by a small child with a bucket.

The north-east corner of the island is defended by **Fort Doyle,** named after General Sir John Doyle, a lieutenant-governor noted for his ambitious public works schemes. The occupying Germans agreed that this was a good place for guns, so they modernized the fort, at the expense of its somewhat romantic 19th-century design.

Beaucette Marina, an all-weather harbour blasted out of the island's bedrock, is occupied by a sleek company of yachts. The place used to be a deep stone quarry, separated from the sea by a relatively narrow wall. Breaching the wall to admit the sea, and boats, turned out to be a big job, but it worked. Because the surrounding land is about 30 feet above sea level, the tops of the masts barely peek above the nearby pastures.

Exporting Guernsey stone was an important industry from the 18th century to the early 20th century; hundreds of disused quarries prove it. In 1775 a public-spirited citizen, John de Havilland, bought an ancient rock pile near the district of Paradis for £4 10s. to save it from the quarrymen. It was a prehistoric passage grave, now called **Le Déhus**. Grass and wild flowers completely cover the mound, which rises as high as the surrounding greenhouses. On one of the dolmen's capstones is a carving thought to represent an archer.

Bordeaux Harbour is popular with fishermen, swimmers and divers. As the tide goes out, hundreds of gulls swarm inches above the sea to waylay the fish left behind in the shallows. To the south you see the ruin of **Vale Castle**, hunched on a hilltop surveying the coast. This spot is believed to have been fortified for the past 2,500 years. The medieval castle,

improved and reinforced over succeeding centuries, was last used by German artillerymen in World War II.

St. Sampson's can hardly be considered a tourist town, though there is some offbeat souvenir shopping. The principal shops face the port and the sea winds, along a compact main street. The boom time for St. Sampson's harbour was the 19th century, when hundreds of thousands of tons of stone were shipped from here to England. Beneath the skyline's cranes and smoking powerplant chimneys, the town has a certain old-fashioned charm. The **Parish Church** is said to be the island's oldest … and looks it. This is reputedly where St. Sampson himself came ashore, bringing Christianity to the 6th-century islanders.

In 1879 a steam tramway line was opened between St. Sampson's and St. Peter Port, about 3 miles to the south. The line skirted **Belle Grève Bay**, a shallow, rocky beach more agreeable for sunbathing and bird-watching than swimming. In 1934 the tramway was driven out of business by the buses. If you don't want to take a bus it's a pleasant enough walk along the bay, with beachside parks and gardens to round out the sea views.

Tomorrow's tomatoes: fatter faster with new glasshouse techniques.

Inland Sights

The pleasures of the interior of Guernsey are close to nature, concentrating as they do on farms, gardens and hidden valleys. Although factory-sized glasshouse complexes occupy much of the countryside, there are still plenty of open pastures, woods and fields of bracken and gorse. Greenhouses have been part of the rural scene here since the end of the 18th century, first for growing grapes, then tomatoes. Now even with diversification into flowers and fruits, a surplus of glass persists. Some redundant greenhouses have been turned into tourist attractions.

With typical Guernsey understatement many of the places worth visiting are hard to find, almost unmarked or hidden around a blind corner. Here are a few to look out for, listed approximately from west to east.

Tropical Vinery, St. Saviour's. Taking advantage of excess greenhouse capacity, this enterprise offers the tourist a bit of escapism. On a chilly day it's a treat to stroll amongst overheated crops of coffee beans and tea leaves, bananas and pineapples, and oriental fruits you may never have heard of.

Reservoir, St. Saviour's. Escapism of quite another sort may be found, free of charge, in the naturally lush countryside surrounding Guernsey's biggest reservoir. You need a

One of the pleasures of roaming the back roads in the Channel Islands: a bargain for impulsive shoppers at a farmer's makeshift fruit stand.

licence to fish here but not to hike through what looks like a classic English landscape painting.

Strawberry Farm, St. Saviour's. Almost anything, it seems, can be grown in Guernsey glasshouses when the Dutch tomato crop becomes too competitive. Here strawberry vines spread out from hanging bags of souped-up soil. After touring the technologically advanced premises you can buy some strawberries to prove that they're good enough to eat. Another glasshouse here has been turned into an aviary, where songbirds thrive in the tropical heat.

Guernsey Tomato Centre, Castel. The romance of greenhouse horticulture is expansively illustrated in this museum under glass. The exhibits start with primitive farming implements and work up to the latest techniques of force-feeding tomatoes in artificial, plastic-bagged soil. In the shop they sell tomato-shaped toys. Single-mindedly, they even bottle tomato wine; you could take home a sample to baffle, or perhaps outrage, your wine-snob friends.

German Occupation Museum, Forest. Beyond a big armoury of German weapons and communications equipment (in almost mint condition), this collection takes into account the human factor. There are woodcarvings done by the occupying soldiers to pass the time, and the instruments on which the German marching band entertained the wary citizens of St. Peter Port. Further reminders of the war years are contained in voluminous files of local propaganda newspapers.

Guernsey Zoo, St. Andrew's. Children are captivated by this zoo specializing in small animals as attractive as tamarins, marmosets and capuchins. More prosaically, there are chipmunks and squirrels, guinea pigs, mice and gerbils. Laughing thrushes and budgerigars provide the music and tethered goats cut the grass.

The Little Chapel (Les Vauxbelets Chapel), St. Andrew's. This curiosity is a favourite of amateur photographers. A scaled-down replica of the church at the Lourdes shrine, it is the third in a series of mini-chapels built in the 1920s by a monk of the de la Salle teaching order. With touching devotion he used almost anything as construction material, decorating it with seashells, broken glass and china. The chapel can accommodate a congregation of half a dozen or more.

German Military Underground Hospital, St. Andrew's. Dank and gloomy, as it must have appeared to the "slave workers" who built it, this is not a "fun" attraction. But a visit to the unfinished Underground Hospital gives a vivid impression of the scope of Hitler's Atlantic Wall programme. More than a mile of corridors and halls were blasted out of the rock. The management keeps a tally of arriving and departing tourists, in case someone gets lost in the dark maze.

Guernsey Folk Museum, Castel. The tall shady trees of Sausmarez Park surround old stables now crammed with authentic stoves, ploughs and carriages of bygone days. Operated by the National Trust of Guernsey, the museum also helps keep alive the ancient Guernsey-Norman patois; exhibits are labelled with their traditional as well as English names.

Le Friquet Butterfly Farm, Castel. Flowers galore are grown commercially · in this complex of greenhouses, but one of the structures is now used as a breeding ground for butterflies. You can walk among the exotic exhibits, as they fly freely through the warm, humid hall. Some of the butterflies are almost as big as bats. Another greenhouse specializes in less lovable insects, such as tarantulas. Added diversions are a restaurant, a souvenir shop, and a croquet lawn with a family of ducks as squatters.

St. Martin's Church, St. Martin's. Construction of this parish church probably began in the 12th century, but the elaborately decorated porch dates from the 15th. What makes this worth a detour is the granite statue at the gate, known as **La Gran'mère du Chimquière.** This life-sized sculpture was carved and polished in the early Bronze Age, perhaps 4,000 years ago. It was further modified to represent a Mother Goddess a couple of thousand years later. The local people of today don't believe in pagan gods, of course. But, to be on the safe side, they sometimes leave offerings of flowers or coins on Grandmother's head. Just for luck.

Guernsey Candles, St. Sampson's. Turning a workshop into a tourist attraction, expert candle-makers display their craft for the visitors. Some of the intricate, hand-carved, multicoloured models are so pretty the wick is only a formality; you'd have to be a Philistine to set one alight.

Oatlands Craft Centre, St. Sampson's. This is a much larger craft centre with a well-conceived layout in a historic setting. Here you can see virtuoso glass-blowers, and clay-throwers at work, and shop for local artefacts ranging from jewellery to patchwork quilts. An educational exhibit devoted to bees and beekeeping includes a video programme plus plenty of "live" action. In the shop below they sell home-made honey and sweet-smelling beeswax candles.

Sausmarez Manor, St. Martin's. Check the schedule with the tourist office before you go, for this lived-in stately home is open to the public only a few hours a week. The manor house has been owned in turn by a successful privateer and his descendant, a general. Another occupant was Sir Edmund Andros, who became governor of the colony of New York in the 17th century. The house was expanded at the turn of the 19th century by Thomas de Sausmarez, who needed more room: his two marriages produced 28 children. The furnishings, from various eras, are worth seeing and include two pianos in the drawing room and a dinner table set for 12. Peacocks and a children's railway enliven the gardens.

Alderney

Once upon a time, people everywhere were as friendly and relaxed as in Alderney. They didn't rush about, or lock their cars or houses, or worry about the air they breathed. In Alderney the excitements are still as basic as bird-watching and beachcombing. So little is happening that the local newspaper appears fortnightly.

The northernmost of the islands, Alderney commands the Channel. You can watch the big ships crowding the horizon. Or the yachts arriving from England or France, having survived some of the world's most complicated sea traffic and tides. The Race, a classically treacherous tidal phenomenon, separates Alderney from France; along the island's north-west coast, the Swinge is only slightly less daunting.

Alderney is only one-fourteenth the size of Jersey. Its permanent population is less than two thousand. It is so small (1,962 acres) that the sea is almost always in view. A reasonably fit hiker can circle the island in a day, along clifftops and beaches, past pastures and forts.

As the island closest to both England and France, Alderney has probably been fortified **75** since Roman times. The biggest British military effort was a chain of 19th-century forts and the overdevelopment of Braye Harbour. In World War II the Germans outdid the Victorians, turning Alderney into a bastion they proudly termed a "battleship of concrete and steel anchored in front of the main Atlantic Wall". The war relics, though ubiquitous, can't undermine the old-fashioned charm.

🐾 St. Anne

Alderney's capital, officially named St. Anne, more usually called "town", is not a seaport. It was established in the centre of the island, meaning a 15-minute walk to the coast, because the local farmers wanted to live close to their fields. The street names are often French, but English is the only language of Alderney; the Norman patois has died out.

St. Anne lacks any ancient or stirring monuments, but the overall effect is thoroughly engaging: pastel-painted old houses along cobbled streets, and a cattle trough in what used to be the main square.

The **Parish Church,** almost as big and august as a cathedral, stands in a forested hillside just off the main street. St. Anne's Church can seat half the population of Alderney. When it was built in the middle of the 19th century, no fund-raising drives were required; it was a gift from the Rev. John Le Mesurier, son of the island's last hereditary governor. The architect borrowed old Norman and early English styles.

Victoria Street, named Rue de Grosnez until a royal visit in 1854, is the main shopping street. But since there aren't enough shops, hotels and restaurants to go around, there's

room enough for private houses, too.

In High Street, perpendicular to Victoria Street, the **Museum** of the Alderney Society occupies an 18th-century schoolhouse. The exhibits cover everything about Alderney from archaeology to World War II. There are photographs and a map of the 24 worst shipwrecks in local waters, an appropriate theme for an island surrounded by dangerous rocks. A separate rock collection shows the geological origins of Alderney. Volunteers answer questions and sell books, postcards and souvenirs.

One of the most elegant places in St. Anne is **Connaught Square.** The **Island Hall** community centre has had a patchy history. Once the home of the hereditary governor and

In High Street, St. Anne, the pace of Alderney life hasn't changed.

ALDERNEY

Fort Les Homeaux Florains

Fort Quesnard

Baie du Grounard

Veaux Trembliers Bay

Fort Corblets

Corblets Bay

Fort Ile de Raz

Chateau à l'Etoc

Longis Bay

Bibette Head

Chateau de Longis

Fort Albert

Essex Castle

Roselle Point

Hanging Rock

La Tchue

Braye Bay

Breakwater

Harbour

Braye

Newtown

Crabby Bay

Fort Doyle

ST. ANNE

Saline Bay

Crabby

Fort Tourgis

Grosse Rock

Airport

Clonque Bay

Fort Clonque

Telegraph Bay

Hannaine Bay

Trois Vaux

Le Puits Jervais

Les Etacs

0   1 km

0   1 mile

later a convent, it served the German army as its *Soldatenheim,* a sort of NAAFI recreation centre. Occupation headquarters was set up across the street in the Royal Connaught Hotel. Because almost the entire civilian population had been evacuated to England before the occupation, the Germans were able to devote themselves uncompromisingly to developing the island as one big military base and prison camp.

In the shadow of Alderney's ugliest war relic, Les Mouriaux tower (a combination water tower, lookout and communications post), is an unorthodox crafts centre, the **Alderney Pottery.** Founded in 1962, it produces handmade pottery from Devon and Dorset clay, often in designs with oriental or medieval English inspiration. In addition, wool is hand spun here and made into individually designed rugs and sweaters.

Braye Harbour

Alderney is the only Channel island with its main port on the north coast. Braye Harbour, in the island's biggest bay, hides behind a monstrous Victorian jetty that mitigates northwesterly gales. As the sea is notoriously destructive here, the Braye Harbour project, begun in 1847, proved immensely costly and only partly successful. The breakwater, originally nearly a mile long, is something of an eyesore, and still needs repairs after every really big storm.

The Admiralty's project took on its own momentum, requiring the construction of a ring of forts to protect the incipient naval base. It all fizzled out after about 30 booming years. Before the Royal Navy "discovered" Braye, it was a busy enough little port, much frequented by privateers and smugglers. The cellars of some of the 18th-century houses near the port were used for storing contraband; nowadays they serve as restaurants and bars in which newly arrived yachtsmen trade tall stories.

Millions of tons of stone were needed to build the Braye breakwater. A railway was run between the quarries and the port. It was all so exciting that Queen Victoria and Prince Albert came to inspect the project's progress, and they were given a train ride.

The **Alderney Railway** is back in business, but only on Sundays, as a tourist trip. Enthusiasts run a steam engine and a more modern diesel on alternate weeks. The excursion from the Braye Road Station to the Mannez Quarry and back takes less than half an hour, allowing a five-minute break to stretch the legs and admire the locomotive. The route, however utilitarian in concept, offers excellent views of the sea, the reservoir and the flower-decked right-of-way. And it's the last railway left in the Channel Islands.

Round the Island

In addition to being the island's commercial, fishing and pleasure port, **Braye Bay** is an ideal beach for bathers and windsurfers, with a gentle sandy slope suitable even for children. At the east end of the bay, settled into the hilltop, **Fort Albert** has fallen into disrepair since its mobilization as a German coastal artillery battery in World War II. When it was built in the 1840's, it was the key fort in the network of British defences facing a presumed threat from France.

Inland, just east of the fort, a **memorial** indicates the varied backgrounds of the "slave workers" who perished in Alderney during the German occupation. Plaques are inscribed in Polish, Hebrew, Russian, French and Spanish. Overwork, beatings and a starvation diet contributed to the deaths of 389 forced labourers and prisoners.

Shipwrecks are among attractions of Alderney's treacherous coast.

Continuing clockwise around the coast, **Saye Bay** (pronounced "soy") is another good sandy children's beach. So is **Corblets Bay,** farther east. Among the many shipwrecks to enter the local folklore was the French sailing ship *Carioca,* lost on the rocks near here in 1866. Some of the cargo—notably a shipment of pianos—sailed ashore in concert.

Fort Corblets, one of the most elegant of the Victorian strongholds, has been transformed into a luxurious if

in the day, considering the number of shipwrecks along this perilous coast. In addition to its 400,000-candlepower light, the inshore tower is equipped with a deafening foghorn. But, lighthouse or no, the wrecks continue. A recent arrival, the container ship *Corinna*, was impaled on the rocks of Quesnard Point, a spectacle for islanders and tourists alike.

Longis Bay is a broad crescent of sand with safe bathing, backed by a vast storm wall, courtesy of the Germans. It keeps the sand from blowing onto the nearby golf course. The wall, with pillboxes, was one big tank trap erected to dissuade the Allies from using this inviting invasion route.

Far below **Essex Castle,** originally a 16th-century fort and now subdivided into fashionable flats, is a natural phenomenon called **Hanging Rock.** An island legend explains this unlovely 50-foot-high tooth of stone rising from the coast: the devil inspired some mischievous Guernseymen to tie their boat to Hanging Rock and try to tow Alderney home. The rock tilted, but, as hard as they rowed, they didn't make it.

Cliffs form the coastline from here westward to Hannaine Bay, nearly halfway around the island. Paths **81**

unconventional private home. To the south looms a three-storey naval direction-finder tower from the German occupation. In an ironic commentary on its bulk and streamlined architecture, the locals call it the Odeon.

The **Mannez Lighthouse** dates from 1912, rather late

The Yellow Birds

Alderney's lifeline is a peppy little airline that carries a quarter of a million passengers per year, plus a few pigs and goats. Most of the flights take 15 minutes or less.

Aurigny Air Services (Aurigny is the old French name for Alderney) is the island's largest private employer. Its pilots come from the big airlines and the RAF. They fly small propellor planes linking the three biggest Channel islands and nearby airports in England and France. The busiest route, between Jersey and Guernsey, schedules 19 flights a day.

There are no refreshments on Aurigny's bright yellow planes, which have neither stewardesses nor aisles. But Aurigny's in-flight magazine contains a diagram of the control panel, for back-seat drivers who enjoy looking over the pilot's shoulder.

among the wild flowers follow the clifftops, revealing the ruggedness of this side of Alderney's nature. The Victorian military planners considered the south coast naturally invulnerable, but the Germans installed a full quota of bunkers. Hikers are warned to stay alert to the danger of concealed dugouts and overgrown barbed wire. The tunnels the Germans dug in various parts of the island are deemed especially treacherous.

The prairie toward the southwest corner of the island accommodates Alderney Airport, with an "A"-shaped layout of airstrips. Only one of them, less than half a mile long, is paved. The oldest airport in the islands, Alderney was opened to commercial traffic in 1935.

The main east–west runway points toward **Les Etacs,** a landing strip of another type. The so-called Garden Rocks, less than a quarter mile offshore, are home to a commuter crush of graceful gannets. The biggest of British seabirds, they nest together almost shoulder to shoulder, and the air is constantly filled with soaring birds returning from fishing trips. (The layman might mistake them for common seagulls, but gannets have black wingtips and a span up to six feet.)

A concrete causeway dated 1942 connects another islet, just offshore, with the "mainland". The islet is occupied by **Fort Clonque,** a bouncily named Victorian strongpoint. For those who really want to get away from it all, Fort Clonque has been converted into tourist flats.

A twisting path called **the**

Zigzag climbs rather laboriously from the causeway to the plateau above. One third of the way up, you can catch your breath, and the sweeping sea view, on a green-and-white bench "given by Dorothy Gyde on her 90th birthday". The inscription doesn't say whether she hiked here for the presentation.

The next of the coastal forts, **Fort Tourgis,** was equipped with 16 heavy cannon in its heyday in the 1880s. Its stately architecture was the victim of World War II "improvements".

Saline Bay, beyond, is a beautiful, spacious swathe of golden sand. The bad news is that it is posted as unsafe for bathing because of a fierce undertow. **Fort Doyle,** at the east end of the bay, has been only partly restored after its service on the Atlantic Wall. Finally, **Crabby Bay,** more pleasant than its name, is just around the corner from the excitements of Braye Harbour.

In the port you can sign up for a 90-minute boat trip circumnavigating Alderney. Weather willing, this is an invigorating way to get a new slant on the island, from hidden caves to wreck sites and a nudist beach. The excursion includes a sidetrip to **Burhou,** a couple of miles offshore. This negligible island has a colony of hundreds of funny-faced puffins as well as some storm petrels. Serious bird-watchers can arrange to stay overnight in the crude hut on the island.

Farther afield, about 7 miles west of Alderney, the reef named **Les Casquets** has been a menace to navigation since the invention of the sail. It was the graveyard for so many ships that a primitive lighthouse was operated there as early as 1724.

During World War II the lighthouse, occupied by the Germans, was raided by British Commandos. They captured all seven German navy men, most of them asleep. A puzzled Commando later reported: "I thought we'd caught a woman, sir. One of them was wearing a hairnet. Honest, sir, a bloody hairnet!"

Today's lighthouse keepers change shifts by helicopter, but in the 19th century there was no relief: one family stayed 19 years without a break. A supply ship came by once a month. According to one contemporary account, an artisan sent to the rock to do repairs fell in love with the keeper's daughter. He invited her to visit him in Alderney, and she finally did. But she soon rushed back to the Casquets; Alderney was too noisy.

Sark

Travellers who never notice flowers or birds suddenly become avid botanists and birdwatchers on the unspoiled island of Sark. Nothing encroaches on nature here, not so much as the sound of a car.

The unpolluted quiet enhances the impression of a paradise island. More prosaically, the Sarkese pay almost no taxes. Luxuries are so cheap that travellers returning to Guernsey are subject to customs controls.

Even if it were not a lush, lovely island, Sark would be worth a visit for its history and social structure. It is a feudal state, still run more or less as decreed by Queen Elizabeth I in the 16th century. The *Seigneur* (lord) of Sark owes allegiance only to the British monarch; the 40 tenants of the feudal lands join 12 elected representatives in an island parliament, called the Chief Pleas. The population numbers less than 600 in a territory of about 2 square miles.

Sark rises steeply from the sea less than 8 miles east of Guernsey—a 35-minute launch trip from St. Peter Port. Day trips to Sark are also feasible from Jersey by hydrofoil. Sark has no airport. Cars and motorcycles are forbidden, but tractors are used for transport as well as farming. Visitors have a choice of touring the island by hired bicycle, horse-drawn carriage, or on foot. With all the winding, unmarked footpaths, it's no disgrace to ask directions, even of another tourist.

Horse-carriage tours of Sark take in the 18th-century Seigneurie.

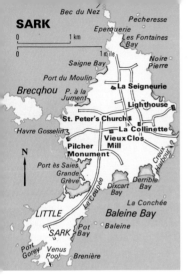

SARK

0   1 km
0   1 mile

Bec du Nez
Pecheresse
Epercuerie
Les Fontaines Bay
Noire Pierre
Saigne Bay
Port du Moulin
Brecqhou
P. à la Jument
La Seigneurie
Lighthouse
St. Peter's Church
La Collinette
Havre Gosselin
Vieux Clos Mill
Pilcher Monument
Creux Harbour
Port ès Saies
Grande Grève
Derrible Bay
Dixcart Bay
La Conchée
LITTLE
Baleine Bay
SARK
Pot Bay
Baleine
Port Gorey
Venus Pool
Brenière
La Coupée
N

The Harbours

Sark's prettiest little port, Creux Harbour, on the east coast, is too shallow for low-tide operation. Most visitors arrive at the modern harbour of La Maseline, a few yards up the coast, which suffers no such handicap. The ports are linked by tunnels through the surrounding cliffs. The old-time fishermen's harbour, *Havre Gosselin,* on the west coast, is especially popular with yachtsmen.

From Le Creux or La Maseline it's a long haul to the plateau on which the village and most of the island's sights are found. The average altitude of the plain is 300 feet above sea level. Fortunately, tractor-drawn buses meet the boats. The road up Harbour Hill, lined with trees and flowers, is such a pleasant, shady route you may decide to savour the return journey on foot.

The Village

The haphazardly arranged little village of Sark consists of a couple of banks, a telephone kiosk, a post box and a handful of shops and houses. The closest thing to a centre of town, **La Collinette** ("the little hill"), is the crossroads separating the banks. Here the horses and carriages stand by for clients. The old drivers are Sarkese, but most of the youngsters (some are girls) come from the U.K. for the season; they have to pass a driving test. In the main street the speed limit is 5 miles per hour. Wandering through the village, tourists nod and smile at each other, as if conspiring in the secret of discovering Sark.

According to a guidebook published in Edinburgh in 1868, **St. Peter's Church** "produces a most disagreeable effect to the eye from every point of view". You may not think so. In any case, the interior of the early 19th-century church is tidy and cheerful, as a fishermen's church ought to be. Plaques on the walls commemorate local citizens lost at sea. Tapestry cushion-covers in the pews show the coats of arms of feudal families; the crossed keys design identifies the pew reserved for prisoners.

The island **prison** is a two-cell model of more or less Romanesque design, dated 1856 in large numerals. To this day it is occasionally put to use as a temporary lockup, to the amusement of pupils in the junior school next door. Two part-time constables maintain Sark's law and order.

Out of Town

In what might be termed the northern suburbs of the village, **La Seigneurie,** Sark's most impressive structure, has been the home of the island's rulers since 1730. If the lord of the manor doesn't invite you to tea, you can still visit the grounds on Wednesdays, Fridays or public holidays. From the high-walled formal garden you get a good look at the front of the grand old granite house, a curious architectural medley containing 16 stairways. In the grounds is a bronze cannon inscribed as a gift from Elizabeth I to the first Seigneur of Sark. Notice, too, the *colombier* or dovecot, still the only one allowed in the island under the feudal regime.

The present Seigneur, Michael Beaumount, an engineer, inherited his domain on the death of his grandmother, Dame Sibyl Hathaway. Her finest hour came during World War II. With her unflappable aristocratic manner and serviceable German, Dame Sibyl faced down the occupation authorities and defended the rights of her people. But she was unable to prevent the deportation of her American-born husband to a prison camp. (Dame Sibyl also spoke *Sercqais,* the Norman-French patois still heard among older islanders. During the war the locals infuriated the occupation forces by communicating in their "secret" language.)

The tallest structure in Sark is the **lighthouse**, hunched halfway down a cliffside at Pointe Robert on the east coast. Tourists are welcome to visit the installation, built in 1912, but there are 146 steps to descend to the base of the lighthouse. Save some breath for the spiral staircase inside the beacon. The 2,800,000-candlepower light can be seen 21 miles away.

On the opposite side of the island, the **Pilcher Monument,** an obelisk on the cliffs above

Havre Gosselin, commemorates one of countless shipwrecks. From this vantage point you can haughtily survey the private island of **Brecqhou**, across a dangerous strait. In the 1960s, a British financier, Leonard Matchan, bought the island, a 160-acre prairie jutting from the sea. Seclusion does not preclude contact with the outside world by telephone and helicopter.

Most of the coast of Sark is a wall of sheer if flower-topped cliffs, but here and there coves and bays soften the coastline. No beach is very easy to reach from the plateau above, but the descent through ferns and foxgloves, bluebells and primroses is refreshing. Here are a few beaches that are safe for bathers.

Grande Grève, on the west coast, is a big sandy bay suitable for children, but a long climb down. **Port du Moulin**, behind the Seigneurie, has spectacular rock formations. On the east side, **Dixcart Bay**, safe and sandy, is divided by an arch of rock, and **Derrible Bay**, in spite of its name, has an attractive beach. Most other beaches are good for sunbathing, rock collecting or cave exploration, but only serious swimmers and divers should take the plunge.

Little Sark

Sark is essentially two islands connected by a narrow isthmus, **La Coupée.** Crossing from Great Sark to Little Sark, over a natural bridge, is an adventure in itself, though not nearly as daring as in olden times. A guidebook writer in 1845, G.W. James, let himself go: "Stranger, look down, if thou canst without giddiness, from these battlements of mouldering rock onto the gulph of stormy waters on either side. Fear not, but cross with steady step; for, in truth, there is no danger, except in hurricanes from the west ... then, indeed, it is rather difficult to keep a firm footing."

In 1945 German prisoners of war were put to work building a proper causeway, which now resembles the Great Wall of China, if only 150 yards long. From the middle of La Coupée there's more heart-stopping scenery in less space than almost anywhere. Directly to left and right, dangerous cliffs drop more than 250 feet, and the horizons reveal Guernsey, Jersey

Inadvertently in dry dock, sailors in Sark enjoy the sunshine and wait for high tide to free them.

Until recent times the road across La Coupée was risky going for brave travellers to Little Sark.

and Normandy. Solid railings on either side provide a sense of security as you take in the view.

You will find Little Sark an even more tranquil world than the main part of the island. It is so quiet you can hear the cows cutting the grass. Gaily coloured wild flowers cascade down the embankments alongside the dusty road.

Toward the south end of Little Sark, proceed carefully among the remains of several stone towers, the melancholy monuments to a 19th-century silver mining venture. It looked promising on paper, and hundreds of Cornish miners were recruited. But they failed to find profitable quantities of any mineral. In 1845 one shaft, burrowed deep under the sea, was flooded, drowning

Herm

The smallest of the Bailiwick of Guernsey's getaway islands, Herm is a beachy farming community with neither taxes nor taxis. No cars, aeroplanes or transistors spoil the peace and quiet. But civilization makes itself felt in constructive ways. There is electricity and running water and, at the harbour, a bright yellow telephone box containing an ancient pay phone with "A" and "B" buttons.

The area of Herm is close to 500 acres. At low tide, though, another thousand acres of sandy beaches and rocky seashore appear. In the 1981 census, the population of Herm attained 37 people. The absolute ruler of this domain is a retired major, Peter Wood, who owns the island's lease until 2029. His title is not Prince or Lord but The Tenant. He owns the hotel, the pub, the shops, the cattle—everything. But he's stopped issuing postage stamps.

With very limited hotel, cottage and camping accommodation available, day-tripping is the only option for perhaps a thousand visitors daily in season. Herm is only about 20 minutes by boat from Guernsey. In spite of the influx of tourists, the tiny island has paths and beaches enough to

ten miners and sinking the whole project. The collapse of the venture impoverished the family of the seigneur, who sold the fief to the first of the present dynasty, Marie Collings, the daughter of a prosperous pirate.

An intriguing direction sign in Little Sark indicates the path "To Venus". This leads to the **Venus Pool**, a rock pool in the corner of Clouet Bay. The water, refreshed with every tide, is deep, clear and inviting.

HERM

N

La Brenière
Port es Valhes
Mouissonnière Beach
La pointe du gentilhomme
Oyster Point
Pierre aux Rats (obelisk)

Le Petit Monceau

Robert's Cross

La Chimquère

La Grand Monceau

La prise à cheval

Shell Beach

The Bear's Beach

Half Tide Causeway

152 Monku

Frenchmans Point

Belvoir Bay

Fishermans Bay
Beacon

Le Manoir

Belvoir House

Herm Harbour

Dairy Farm

Cauchie de Robert

Rosière Steps

Puffin Bay

Moie Sercq
Pointe du Ségard

Bishops Cove

Barbara's Leap

Pt. Sauzebourge

0   200   400 m
0   200   400 yards

absorb the crowds; what they want, after all, is scenery, silence and solitude.

Arriving at Herm

The brief boat ride from St. Peter Port crosses the Little Russel passage, studded with rocky hazards. They are no problem for the ferrymen or yachtsmen, who follow beacons designating the safe route. One startling sight along the way is a big cylindrical Victorian fort on its own miniature island. This is the brooding **Bréhon Tower,** which saw action during World War II as a German anti-aircraft base; it is reputed to have scored a 50 percent success rate, shooting down one Allied plane and one Luftwaffe.

Herm Harbour suffers from the chronic Channel tidal problem: at low tide it's a wading pool. If you arrive when the harbour is not receiving, your boat will land a quarter of a mile to the south, at the **Rosière Steps.** Either way, simply follow the path to the stone cottages of the **Harbour Village.** In a central *piazza,* built by Italian workers in 1963, pastel-painted buildings cater to most tourist needs. In the hotel grounds is a windowless **jail** barely big enough for one prisoner, built of granite in

1826. It is said to be the smallest jail in the world.

The gift shops sell exotic coral specimens and shell necklaces; all come from the Philippines. You can collect your own shells, just as pretty, for nothing, at Herm's Shell Beach. The only home-made products on sale are in the pottery line—coffee mugs and plates, for instance. Philatelists will want to buy a packet of Herm stamps, no longer valid but no less prized. (Guernsey stamps must be used on all outgoing mail.)

Unlike the mysterious sister islands, where getting lost is part of the fun, Herm is meticulously signposted. The signs even tell how many minutes it should take to walk where you're going. It's logical, for everyone is a pedestrian here.

Around the Island

Heading north from the village, the footpath winds between the honeysuckle and the sea. **Fisherman's Beach** is an ideal spot for sunbathing. Beyond that, the path skirts a tiny **cemetery,** actually not much bigger than a "king-sized" bed. It's a reminder of a cholera epidemic of 1832; these victims were passengers on a passing ship.

Here the path forks; the inland route crosses the grass and dunes of the **Common,** a haunt of rabbits since the days of the Normans. At Robert's Cross you can see what's left of a **prehistoric tomb,** a neolithic passage grave 16 feet long. A crude obelisk a quarter mile north of here marks the spot where a large prehistoric menhir stood; in the 19th century, quarrymen exported it as just another hunk of granite.

Much of the east coast of Herm is occupied by the dazzling expanse of **Shell Beach,** which flashes in the sun and can be spotted by sailors many miles away. Through a quirk of the tides, shells from hundreds and perhaps thousands of miles away gravitate to this beach. So do sunbathers and swimmers. Conchologists go wild over Painted Tops, Dwarf Winkles, Hunchback Scallops and Warty Venus, and people who never notice seashells suddenly bend over and become collectors. A café overlooking the beach sells a guide to the 50 most interesting shells. The dunes behind support prickly sea holly, marram grass and burnet roses.

Continuing clockwise around the island, **Belvoir Bay** is a small, sandy, perfectly sheltered beach. Inland, and up a steep, shaded path, is **Le Manoir,** the *real* village where 93 the islanders live and work. Here there is an unobtrusive power station, a school, a workshop, cottages and The Tenant's home. What appears to be a medieval keep was built within the past century by a tenant with a feeling for history, Prince Blücher. A genuine medieval building, though, is the 11th-century **chapel** dedicated to an unfamiliar saint, St. Tugual. There is a separate bell tower.

In the fields surrounding the manor, Herm's dairy herd

grazes above the sea. The cows, registered Guernseys, produce more than 200 gallons of milk per day—for export to Guernsey.

A cliff path leads past **Barbara's Leap**, from where a young woman fell and, amazingly, survived. From the southern extremity of Herm, **Sauzebourg Point**, you look down on the flat-topped private island of **Jethou.** Legend says the two islands were connected until the 8th century, when a great storm split them asunder. Jethou has an area of about 44 acres, and a couple of offshore islands of its own, popular with puffins.

They stoop to conch collecting: seaweedy scene on Shell Beach.

A Day in France

The Channel Islands are so close to Normandy and Brittany that excursions to France are easy. There are day-long package tours by boat, hydrofoil or airplane; or you can do it yourself, for a day or a week. With all the sightseeing, shopping and, of course, French cuisine, there's never enough time for everything, but you do get a look at another way of life, quite different from that on the adjacent British islands. You'll need your passport. Here, in a nutshell, are some of the day-trip destinations offered by various Channel Islands travel agencies, reading approximately from west to east.

Dinard. This fashionable town has enjoyed over a century of glory since its "discovery" by Anglo-American travellers in the 1850s. A broad sheltered beach, one of the best in northern Brittany, a particularly mild micro-climate—palm, fig trees, tamarisk and camellias flourish here—and easy access across the Channel make it an obvious favourite. Dinard has all the elements of the perfect resort: luxury villas, long paved promenades, plush hotels, smart shops, a "serious" casino, parks and gardens, discotheques and an Olympic swimming pool. A faintly Victorian atmosphere persists, adding to Dinard's appeal.

Dinan. Towering above the River Rance, this delightful town behind stone ramparts brings to life medieval Brittany. The sagging, cantilevered, wood-fronted houses, leaning crazily on each other, today house butcher's shops, pharmacies and the workshops of artisans. Beyond the maze of flower-decked cobbled streets is a 14th-century castle; the dungeon is now a museum. The collection includes splendid examples of Breton furniture and costumes.

Saint-Malo. Conscientiously restored after wartime destruction, the old walled city of noble stone houses lives anew. In the high season, group tours of the ramparts encircling the town run every hour and are well worth taking. The walls, built in the 12th century and altered over and over again until the 18th, command superb vistas out over the sea, the beaches and, inwards, over the town itself.

Between Saint-Philippe bastion and Tour Bidouane, the whole Emerald Coast opens up: the Rance Estuary, with, way in the distance, Cap Fréhel, and somewhat nearer,

Dinard beach. In front lie the islets of Grand-Bé, Petit-Bé and Cézembre: at low tide you can walk or wade to Grand-Bé for the views out over the ocean and to visit the simple tomb of François-René de Chateaubriand, the Romantic writer, who chose to be buried here. Don't forget to return as soon as the tide turns—or you may find yourself trapped!

A popular attraction lies just below the steps beside Porte Saint-Thomas: the **Aquarium**, where fauna from the seas all around frolic in tanks built right into the ramparts.

The tower of **Quic-en-Groigne** houses an interesting **waxworks museum**, recounting the history of Saint-Malo and bringing vividly to life the colourful swashbuckling characters of times past. More relics and reminders of old Saint-Malo are on view in the **Musée d'Histoire de la Ville**, just across Place Chateaubriand. Exhibits, mostly with a seafaring angle, include everything from sailors' trunks to colossal ships' figureheads.

Brimming over with hotels and cafés, **Place Chateaubriand** is a good place to take a break. From here head on into the centre through a delightful maze of streets to the **Cathédrale Saint-Vincent**, begun in the 12th century and heavily restored after the last war. The openwork tower rising way above the walls is visible from far and wide.

Cancale. This pretty port, with small fishermen's houses skirting the harbour, means oysters, oysters galore, oysters sold individually *(au détail)* or in great baskets *(bourriches)*. Follow your nose down to the stalls on the beach; all around, oyster beds stretch off into the muddy distance. The main square has a profusion of restaurants—oyster and fish restaurants, naturally.

Mont Saint-Michel. Often called "Wonder of the Western World", the abbey-fortress remains long in the memory, for its setting atop a rocky hill with a vast sandy bay all around, for its incomparably fine architecture, for its history and the sheer magnitude of the achievement.

It all started in the 8th century, when Aubert, Bishop of Avranches, had a vision in which the Archangel Michael commanded him to build an oratory on the island of Tombe. Soon pilgrims were drawn to the place and new buildings had to be put up. Fired by a spirit of faith, Benedictine monks set about the task, and in 1017 work on the abbey proper began. Building spurted ahead early in the 13th century with the construction of the almonry, Knights' Hall, refectory and cloisters, known collectively as the Marvel *(la Merveille)*. Defences were put up, mostly in the 14th century, followed by a grandiose Flamboyant Gothic replacement for the chancel of the church, which collapsed in 1421.

Most visitors approach the Mont via the half-mile-long causeway constructed in 1874. But the pilgrims of old made their way here at low tide, traversing the treacherous quicksands left by the receding sea. Today threatened by a silting up of the bay, Mont-Saint-Michel is an island only during moon tides when the sea rises at a rate of nearly 50 yards a minute, covering a distance of 10 miles or so. Prudence is the order of the day for those who wish to follow the pilgrims' route: fogs can come up all of a sudden, and it's easy to lose your bearings.

To visit the abbey, you have to join one of the multilingual guided tours, which take just under an hour. As you wander up and down through a confusing progression of rooms, remember that the abbey complex occupies three distinct levels, situated one on top of another: the *lower*, with storeroom and almonry; the *middle*, site of the Knights' Hall and Guest Hall, and the *upper*, given over to the church, cloister and refectory.

The visit starts from the terrace on top, with superb views of the bay and church façade, and works downwards. The **abbey church** offers striking contrasts between the rugged simplicity of the Romanesque nave and the elegant dynamism of the Flamboyant Gothic chancel, while the **cloister,** with its delicate columns and tiny garden, is a sheer marvel of lightness and grace.

The **refectory** has perfect acoustics, which enabled every monk to follow the lessons that were read amid the clatter of cutlery. Note, too, its unique lighting system. No less impressive are the **Crypte des Gros-Piliers**, with its ten massive pillars, and the **Knights' Hall** *(Salle des Chevaliers),* one of the finest Gothic halls in the world.

Granville. A family resort on Normandy's west coast, with beach and casino. The Lower Town also contains a large commercial port and business centre. In the Upper Town, high above, are fine 19th-century houses, a church begun in the 15th century, and extensive ramparts.

What to Do

Sports

From athletics to water polo, from archery to windsurfing, something is always going on in the Channel Islands. Sports lovers of almost all persuasions are well catered for on the sea and ashore, with both outdoor and indoor facilities. If yours is a "minority" sport like fencing or karate, the tourist office will probably be able to direct you to a local club so you can keep in practice; all you have to do is ask.

Water Sports

Swimming. Swimming in the Channel Islands is an inviting and invigorating diversion in summer. Several of the beaches are as beautiful as you'll find on any sea. But keep in mind the tides, which rise with startling speed, and the danger of submerged rocks. Knowledgeable swimmers also choose a sheltered beach, according to the day's wind direction. A few of the most popular beaches are provided with lifeguards, but generally safety must be your own concern. Most of the accessible beaches are equipped with amenities like cafés and toilets.

Scuba diving. Tuition is available. Experienced divers can go out with local clubs in expeditions to fish-thronged cliffs and rocks, or to sunken war relics. The undersea visibility tends to be best in late spring and summer. As the currents are always tricky, local advice and assistance are essential.

Surfing. The best-known venue in the islands is St. Ouen's Bay, Jersey, where the rollers are up to championship standards. Boards and wetsuits may be hired and professional instructors are available. Guernsey's top surfing beach is Vazon Bay.

Windsurfing. On breezy days they skim across the bays at breathtaking speed. If the world's fastest-growing sport appeals to you, qualified instructors in Jersey, Guernsey and Alderney offer expert tuition for children, beginners and accomplished windsurfers. Guernsey's Cobo Bay is where Prince Charles learned windsurfing in the 1970s.

Water-skiing. Jersey's busiest water-ski school meets at La Haule slipway in St. Aubin's Bay; equipment and instruc-

Scuba divers gingerly take to the ocean at Jersey's Bouley Bay.

MRS. M. E. RIVE - FROM HER FRIENDS - 1980

Improvised parking accommoda-
tion for rented bikes on isle of Sark.

tion are also available at St.
Brelade's Bay. Guernsey's water-
ski activities are concentrated at
Havelet Bay, St. Peter Port.

Sailing. For beginners, Jersey is best organized for hiring
a dinghy and learning the
ropes. Experienced sailors can
charter yachts from companies
in Jersey or Guernsey and sail
to other islands or France ... or
discover hidden coves closer to
home. If you're sailing your own
boat to the Channel Islands
you'll find a warm welcome
100 and all facilities in the marinas

of Jersey and Guernsey or
Braye Harbour, Alderney. But
note that the seas around
Alderney are extremely treacherous.

Fishing. A wealth of fishing
experiences are available from
beach or breakwater, on a boat
inshore or over a wreck; even
freshwater fishing is pursued
in reservoirs and abandoned
quarries. Deep-sea outings
leave from the principal harbours. Because of the Channel's
mighty tides and the islands'
location, an exceptional variety
of species may be hooked almost anywhere. British records
in many categories belong to
island anglers.

Sports Ashore

Golf. Top British and European players compete in the Jersey Open in June. For non-champions, booking is strongly advised at Jersey's two 18-hole courses (requiring temporary club membership) and two 9-hole public courses. Guernsey's 18-hole seaside course is available for temporary membership, as is the 9-hole course of the St. Pierre Park hotel. Alderney has a scenic 9-hole course used by residents and visitors alike.

Horse riding. Down tree-lined paths, across open fields or along the sand, riding is never dull in Jersey and Guernsey. Various riding schools have instructors, horses and ponies standing by for trekking and hacking.

Tennis. The biggest concentration of courts is at the Jersey Recreation Grounds and at Fort Regent. In Guernsey, start at the Beau Séjour Leisure Centre.

Motor racing. The vast beach at St. Ouen's Bay, Jersey, is the scene of fortnightly races by motorcycles and racing cars. In Guernsey, similiar excitements centre on Vazon Bay.

Other sports. All the traditional British sports, notably football, rugby and cricket, are popular in the islands. Curiously, Guernsey is keen on the American game of softball, a relaxed version of baseball. Jersey revives old-time horse racing eight or nine times a season at Les Landes, high above the sea.

Shopping

The Channel Islands are not a duty-free zone, but they're the next best thing. Duties are very low and Value Added Tax is nonexistent. The biggest bargains glitter among luxury items like jewellery, perfume and cosmetics. But you can't buy everything in sight, for you'll have to go through customs on the way home. (See page 118.)

What to Look For

Alcohol. The prices in the shop windows do the selling on all manner of wines and spirits. By way of an alcoholic souvenir, consider the liqueurs produced in Jersey and Guernsey using the rich local cream.

Ceramics. The islands have potteries you can visit where you are able to watch craftsmen turning out hand-finished pots, vases and crockery. There are shops on the premises.

Clothing. French day-trippers rush for the British chain stores for reasonably priced clothes. With the VAT missing, you may, too.

Flowers. Carnations, roses, freesias or other island-grown flowers are inexpensive for carrying home or posting to friends by overnight delivery.

Jewellery. Minus luxury taxes, expensive jewellery looks more of a bargain; unadorned gold chain is sold here by the yard.

Knitwear. Though most of them are commercially produced, the familiar square-cut fishermen's sweaters carry on a proud tradition. The easiest way to tell them apart: jerseys have an anchor design knitted on the front, but guernseys don't.

Perfumes. All the chic French brands of perfumes and cosmetics are on sale at seductive prices. For souvenir value, consider the island-made scents based on local wild flowers.

Stamps. Philatelists are drawn to the main post offices in Jersey and Guernsey, where definitive sets and special issues from the respective bailiwicks are sold.

Tobacco. Smokers light up when they see the low prices; the best Cuban cigars are considered a big, fat bargain, even at £3 apiece.

Unusual souvenirs. Islanders produce intricately shaped candles, miniature milk cans in copper, and "stone mushrooms" in the form long used to stack corn, now available in miniature to keep your garden gnomes company. Not to forget walking sticks made of the stalks of Jersey giant cabbages.

Window-shoppers smile at Channel Islands' VAT-free price tags.

102

Entertainment

The bigger the island, the livelier and more varied the nightlife.

Jersey offers something for all generations. The young crowd can rock to live bands or international disco sounds, while the older celebrants let their hair down at sing-alongs and cabarets. At the height of the season big name entertainers share the limelight at Fort Regent and the top hotels. Pubs often feature live entertainment, from jazz and folk to amateur nights. Plays and musical varieties take the stage at the old Opera House in St. Helier.

Guernsey has fewer night clubs, discos and musical pubs than Jersey but they come in all the customary varieties from rip-roaring to sedate, from casual to rather posh. Most of the dances and cabarets are found in the big hotels. Look for outdoor barbecue parties and jazz performances, too.

The Beau Séjour Leisure Centre is also a venue for dramas, cabarets and concerts.

In Alderney most of the excitement is found in the pubs and inns. The island enjoys liberal licensing hours, including relatively uninhibited Sundays.

Festivals

Both Jersey and Guernsey stage lavish spectacles in August: the Battle of Flowers carnivals. Fantasy floats are confected of a million carnations, marigolds, hydrangeas and thistles. The Jersey affair, dating back to 1902, is considerably more elaborate. The islands also put on various tournaments and agricultural shows.

Alderney Week, in August, consists of parades, sports events and unusual competitions. Alderney's other festival, in May, is called Milk-a-Punch Sunday. Tradition decrees that the pubs serve a rich rum-and-milk punch, free ... to the regulars, anyway.

Sark's festivals have a rural slant: cattle show in July, garden and agricultural show in August, horse show in September.

Jersey farmers fire a salvo in
104 *their blooming Battle of Flowers.*

Eating Out

Whether you lean toward sophisticated gourmet fare or homespun cooking, you'll eat heartily in the Channel Islands. From genuine *haute cuisine* to ploughman's lunches, pork pies and pizzas, every taste is satisfied.

Best of all are the fresh ingredients—today's fish, new potatoes, juicy tomatoes, and the rich local milk and cream.

Island restaurateurs take great pride in their work. At Jersey's annual culinary competition, crowds of locals turn out just to look at the artfully arranged food, while the cooks worry and the judges have all the fun.

As for atmosphere, name your mood: intimate candlelight or an outdoor setting beside the sea; a *trattoria* or the mysterious orient... or takeaway fish and chips. Many hotels and pubs offer reasonably priced bar lunches.

Fish and seafood take top billing in the islands. Your best bet is the fresh catch listed on the blackboard outside a res-

taurant—lobster or crab, or sea bass, sole or brill. Despite the sea's proximity, they tend to be pricey. A local delicacy, now rare, is the large univalve called an ormer (or if you prefer its formal title, call for *Haliotis tuberculata)*. The ormer, which resembles abalone, requires lengthy preparation. After removal from its shell, the animal is scrubbed, beaten and rubbed with flour. It is fried in butter, then stewed for several hours until tender.

Among meat dishes are versions of the highly regarded local pork. Neither Jersey nor Guernsey cows are beef producers. But you'll find no shortage of restaurants serving roast beef with Yorkshire pudding, green peas, and both boiled and roast potatoes.

Jersey new potatoes—Jersey Royals, as the producers proudly bill them—really are a treat, positively delicious in any context, but preferably with butter and parsley or mint. Other Channel Islands vegetables win much praise: cauliflowers, celery and courgettes. Succulent tomatoes and kiwifruit are mass-produced under glass in Guernsey.

Channel Islands milk, the source of butter the colour of wild buttercups, is incomparably rich. But it is not apt

Sophisticated seafood array makes gala feast of Channel harvest.

for cheesemaking, so you may want to settle for Camembert or Pont-l'Evêque from across the way in Normandy. From neighbouring Brittany comes the recipe for the delicate pancakes *(crêpes)* made in specialist restaurants. Channel Islands cream, as thick as cheese, tops many a calorific dessert.

Native delicacies

Baked beans are one of the few traditional island dishes to have survived into modern times. Originally a Sunday breakfast special, the old-time bean jar contains several kinds of beans plus pork, onions and herbs.

Conger soup, built around one of the least handsome of

How to gild the strawberry: add a dollop of fresh Jersey cream.

Jersey's 'Earlies'

Unlike ordinary new potatoes, Jersey Royals are almost shamelessly delicious. They never taste better than in Jersey itself, in May or June, freshly lifted from the rich soil, washed, boiled, and eaten skin and all. You'd have to be heartless to fry them.

Potatoes have been grown in Jersey since the late 18th century, but it took the development of the Jersey Royal in the 1880's to propel the island into the front rank of producers. The same species is grown elsewhere under the less ringing name of International Kidneys. The delicate Royals are by far Jersey agriculture's most profitable export.

sea monsters, is enhanced with milk and butter, cabbage, leeks and marigold petals.

You will hear about, but probably not get to taste, black butter, a preserve the islanders have made for the last several hundred years. Concocted from apples, sugar, lemons, liquorice and cider, it used to require 24 hours of nonstop work to produce.

Local pastry is worth sampling. The Jersey Wonder is a variation on the doughnut, twisted into a figure of eight. *Fiottes* are balls of sweet pastry poached in milk, usually eaten at Easter. The Guernsey *gâche* is a concentrated fruit cake.

Drinks

Cider was the islanders' favourite drink from the era of the Normans to relatively recent times. Now local production is quite limited, and Channel tipplers are more likely to ask for a pint of bitter or lager. Thanks to the islands' humane tax policy, beer is cheap; the consumers show their gratitude by drinking ever more of it. Bargain prices also encourage the consumption of French wines and liqueurs. All the familiar brands of non-alcoholic beverages are available throughout the archipelago.

How to Get There

Because of the complexity and variability of the many fares, you should consult an informed travel agent well before your trip.

From the U.K.

BY AIR: Dozens of British airports, from Aberdeen to Southampton, have daily direct services to Jersey and Guernsey throughout the summer season (usually April 1 to October 31). Advanced Purchase Excursion (APEX) fares are widely available, cutting costs for travellers who are able to book in advance. Some APEX fares involve weekend supplements, and there are stiff penalties for cancellation. In winter service is greatly reduced, though daily flights are maintained from Southampton, Manchester, Plymouth, Bournemouth, and London's Heathrow and Gatwick airports.

Small planes serve Alderney from Brighton, Bournemouth and Southampton daily during the season; and there are many daily connecting flights between Alderney and the two bigger islands.

Package tours: Travel agents offer a variety of all-inclusive tours to the islands combining reduced-rate flights, scheduled or charter, with accommodation.

BY SEA: Several passenger-and-car ferries link English ports with Jersey and Guernsey. The two south coast ports are Weymouth and Portsmouth, and there is a weekly service from Torquay in the summer.

From Europe

BY AIR: Among European airports linked to the Channel Islands by scheduled flight are Amsterdam, Frankfurt, Zurich, Paris and the Breton town of Dinard (serving Saint-Malo). Winter service, though greatly reduced, includes daily Paris flights.

BY SEA: Fast hydrofoils (passengers only) run between Saint-Malo and Jersey, Guernsey, Alderney, Herm and Sark. Car ferries link the two main islands with both Saint-Malo and Cherbourg. Other ships serve the islands from the Normandy ports of Carteret and Portbail.

From North America

The most efficient route is via either of the principal London airports, Heathrow or Gatwick, from which frequent daily flights serve both Jersey and Guernsey.

When to Go

High season, when fine weather usually compensates for the higher prices, extends from the beginning of June to the middle of September. Some visitors, though, prefer the more economical "shoulder" seasons—from the end of April (when the spring flowers bloom) to the beginning of summer; or September and October (before the sea has cooled). At Christmas time the tourists return, and there are many special events. Jersey and Guernsey vie for the top of the British "sunshine league", averaging around eight hours a day of sun during a typical summer. Rainfall is moderate—about 34 inches a year, falling mostly in the winter. Sea temperatures average around 17 °C in summer. Mean daily temperatures at St. Helier, Jersey (30-year average):

	J	F	M	A	M	J	J	A	S	O	N	D
Temperature °C	6	6	8	10	13	15	17	17	16	13	9	7
Rainfall (mm.)	96	77	66	50	53	42	43	57	73	79	115	111

Planning Your Budget

Because of transport costs, the prices of many everyday items are higher in the Channel Islands than in the United Kingdom, but luxury goods tend to be considerably cheaper, reflecting the island tax situation. To give you an idea of what to expect, here are some average prices. They can only be *approximate,* however, because of relentless inflation.

Accommodation. *Double hotel room* with bath, bed, breakfast and dinner £15–60 per person per day. *Guest house* (some without private bath) £9–16 per person per day. *Self-catered flat* £45–190 per week.

Admissions. Jersey Underground Hospital £2, Zoo £2; most other attractions and museums £1 or less.

Boat trips. Jersey–Sark day-return £12. Guernsey–Herm return £3. Guernsey–Sark day-return £7.40.

Buses. St. Helier to Jersey Zoo 59p. St. Helier to Jersey Airport 70p. St. Peter Port to Beau Séjour 30p. St. Peter Port to Lihou Island 55p.

Bicycle hire. £2 daily, £12 weekly; tandem hire at twice the price.

Car hire. Jersey: *Metro, Nova* or *Fiesta* £10 daily, £60 weekly high season; £9 daily, £54 weekly mid-season; £8 daily, £46 weekly low-season. Guernsey prices approximately £2–3 per day cheaper. Unlimited mileage on all islands.

Cigarettes. 55p for packet of 20.

Dry-cleaning. Jacket £1.70, dress £1.90, skirt £1.40.

Entertainment. Cinema admission £2.50. Nightclub cover charge £2–3.

Hairdressers. *Man's* haircut £3–5. *Woman's* cut £3–4, wash and blow-dry £5.

Meals and drinks. Pub lunch £2. Dinner in good restaurant (à la carte) £8–12. Bottle of wine £4. Pint of beer 55p.

Sports. Windsurfing £4 per hour, scuba diving £11 including tuition and equipment (two hours), deep-sea fishing expedition £5 per person including equipment; golf £2.10 per round, tennis £3 per hour court hire, horseback riding £5–6 per hour.

Taxi. Jersey airport to St. Helier £4. Ferry terminal to St. Aubin £3.50. Guernsey airport to St. Peter Port £3.

BLUEPRINT for a Perfect Trip

An A-Z Summary of Practical Information and Facts

Contents

A **ACCOMMODATION.** (See also CAMPING.) From the simplest guest-house to the kind of hotel that hides from the crowds in the midst of its own park or golf course, Jersey and Guernsey offer accommodation to meet almost every budget and taste. All establishments are inspected and classified according to the level of amenities, facilities and services provided. The grading systems are as complex as they are stringent, although Jersey's is being simplified. At the moment, in Jersey, "first register" **hotels** are awarded from four to one "suns" in descending order of excellence; below them come the less elaborate "second register" establishments (which are sub-classified by between four and one "diamonds"). Guernsey awards registered hotels from five to one crowns. **Guest houses** are rated as grade A, B or C (down to D in Guernsey). Most hotels and guest houses include bed, breakfast and dinner in the terms.

Self-catering flats, whether luxurious or spartan, are rare in Jersey but widely available in Guernsey. They are graded A, B, C or D.

Both Jersey and Guernsey issue official, comprehensive booklets with full lists of all registered hotels, guest houses and self-catering flats and chalets. They cover a multitude of details about each establishment—prices and recreational facilities, for example, and whether dogs and children are welcome. Reservations may be made through qualified travel agents or directly with the hotel or guest house. Tourists who arrive without reservations will find assistance at the airports of Jersey and Guernsey and in the tourist offices at the principal seaports, St. Helier and St. Peter Port.

Alderney, with far fewer tourist facilities than its big neighbours, inspects and approves its hotels, guest houses and holiday flats but does not classify them. Alderney issues its own list of hotels; the other islands of the bailiwick—Sark and Herm—are included in the Guernsey booklet.

AIRPORTS. The biggest of the Channel Islands airports, in Jersey, is small and friendly by most standards, yet counts as the United Kingdom's fourth busiest in terms of traffic. The terminal has shops, a restaurant, bar and buffet, hire-car desks and a tourist information bureau. Buses and taxis provide transport to St. Helier, 5 miles away.

Guernsey airport, even more modern, has a similar range of shops and services. Buses and taxis are available.

Both Jersey and Guernsey airports have "duty-free" shops featuring the favourite island bargains—spirits and cigarettes—and shops
114 selling locally grown fresh flowers to carry away.

Alderney is the only Channel Islands airport with three runways—but two of them are grass. Only short-takeoff planes can use the field, which is a mere ten-minute walk from the centre of town. But there are taxis on hand and hire-cars may be ordered.

BABY-SITTERS. (See also CHILDREN.) Many hotels have a "baby listening service"—a microphone in the bedroom which you can activate when you want the reception desk to monitor a child's sleep. Human baby-sitters are harder to find, though some hotel employees may be available.

BICYCLE and MOPED HIRE. If you aren't deterred by the vagaries of the Channel weather, a bicycle is a sound vehicle for sightseeing. Though you may feel surrounded by cars at times, their drivers are considerate. And the hills are quite surmountable for anyone who is reasonably fit. Bikes may be rented by the day or week; rates include insurance. A deposit will probably be required.

Mopeds (50cc motorbikes) and, in some places, larger motorcycles may be hired by the day or week. A driving licence is required. A helmet, provided by the rental firm, must be worn.

CAMPING. It's forbidden to import trailers and motor caravans. Otherwise, feel free to bring your own tent, or rent one at an authorized camping site. It may not be lavish but will have at least minimal conveniences. Pitching a tent just anywhere—on a beach or farmland—is not allowed.

CAR HIRE. (See also DRIVING.) International and local car-hire firms compete in Jersey and Guernsey, handling thousands of cars of all sizes and prices. Small local firms operate in Alderney, which has relatively few roads. Tariffs in Guernsey and Alderney are significantly below the Jersey scale, in consideration of the relative size of the islands; unlimited mileage is standard everywhere. The rates include liability insurance. Personal injury insurance for you and your passengers may be added. Payment may usually be made by recognized credit card or by cheque backed by a banker's card. Requirements vary slightly from company to company, but in general you must have a valid driving licence and at least one year's driving experience. Many firms impose a minimum age limit of 20 years, though younger drivers are accepted if they take out supplementary insurance. Some companies have a maximum age (69) as well.

C Local drivers give a wide berth to hired cars, which are instantly identifiable by the number plate, emblazoned with a big letter "H" on a brightly coloured background. (Islanders jeer that the "H" stands for "Horrible"—the way they accuse some "foreign" motorists of driving.)

CHILDREN. Some hotels welcome children and say so in the official island brochures listing facilities. Playpens, cots and high-chairs may be rented by the week. All the islands have abundant attractions for children of all ages, starting with immense sandy beaches. Jersey's world famous zoo is a memorable treat for youngsters; Guernsey's zoo, though a minor-league establishment, is geared for children. Both islands have butterfly farms, strawberry farms and artisans to watch. For rainy days there are amusements at Jersey's Fort Regent and Guernsey's Beau Séjour leisure centres.

CIGARETTES, CIGARS, TOBACCO. The punitive taxes levied against smoking in most of the world do not apply in the Channel Islands, where tobacco is one of the notable bargains. A big selection of British and foreign brands of cigarettes, cigars and pipe tobacco is available in specialist shops.

Smoking is prohibited in buses. Many taxis now post "no smoking" signs, as well. A few hotels reserve certain rooms for non-smokers.

CLIMATE and CLOTHING. Even if you're heading for the Channel Islands in mid-summer, take a sweater for those chilly nights by the sea. Better yet, buy one on the spot—a jersey, guernsey or alderney. The odds indicate you might need an umbrella, too. But don't be discouraged by these cautions; bathing suits also deserve priority.

All the islands have coastlines and country paths to intrigue ramblers and hikers, so take along appropriate shoes or boots.

As for formality: topless sunbathing is permissible on the beaches (if discreet) but is not encouraged, and bathing suits are inappropriate in the towns. Casual wear, even shorts for women, is all right during the daytime. Nightclubs and discos usually outlaw jeans, and many a pub simply announces, "No shirt, no beer". In better restaurants men are expected to wear jacket and tie for dinner.

COMMUNICATIONS

Post offices and mail. Jersey's pillar boxes are red; Guernsey's are blue. Each bailiwick runs its own post office and issues its own stamps. United Kingdom stamps are not valid on outgoing mail. Leaving Jersey, mail must bear Jersey postage, and from Guernsey, Alderney, Sark or Herm only Guernsey stamps are valid. The postage rates are below U.K. levels and the service is fast—barring fog which occasionally grounds a mail plane. The main post offices in St. Helier and St. Peter Port have philatelic bureaux with local stamps for sale to collectors and exhibitions for everyone. There are sub-post offices in each parish. The Alderney post office is a sub-office of Guernsey.

Poste restante. If you're not sure which hotel you'll be staying in, you can receive mail c/o Poste Restante at the main post office. You'll need identification to pick up your letters.

International telegrams may be sent by telephone, dictating the text to the operator (dial 100 for assistance).

Telephone. Jersey Telecoms and Guernsey Telecoms run up-to-date, efficient services at relatively low prices. Public telephones, in their bright yellow kiosks, come with full instructions for their sophisticated operation. From any coin-box telephone you can direct-dial to the U.K., Ireland, and much of the rest of the world. Dialling a number yourself, instead of having the operator intervene, saves money. It's easy and cheap to dial from one Channel Island to another.

COMPLAINTS. Problems with accommodation can, and should, be worked out face to face, but if this fails you should turn to the Tourism Department in Jersey or, in Guernsey, the Hotel Inspector's Office next to the tourist office in St. Peter Port.

In Guernsey, complaints about buses or taxis must be presented in writing to the States Passenger Transport Licensing Authority, St. Peter Port.

CONSULAR OFFICES. Citizens of Belgium, France, Italy, West Germany, the Netherlands, Portugal and the Scandinavian countries who have problems in the Channel Islands may find a sympathetic ear at their consular offices. Check the telephone directory. And most nationalities are represented by full-scale consulates in London.

CRIME and THEFT. Although the crime rate in the islands is low, it's unwise to tempt fate by leaving valuables in view in a parked car. Tourists themselves sometimes break the law in the form of motoring contraventions (the very low speed limits take some getting used to).

C **CUSTOMS and ENTRY FORMALITIES.** Citizens of Britain and the Irish Republic do not require passports or visas for travel to the Channel Islands. Citizens of the European Community countries plus Austria, Switzerland, Monaco and Liechtenstein may enter with either passports or national identity cards. Nationals of other Western European countries, and North America, need valid passports but no visa.

The following chart shows the main duty-free items you may take into Britain and, when returning home, into your own country:

Into:	 Cigarettes	 Cigars	 Tobacco	 Spirits	 Wine
Britain	400 or	100 or	500 g.	1 l. and	2 l.
Australia	200 or	250 g. or	250 g.	1 l. or	1 l.
Canada	200 and	50 and	900 g.	1.1 l. or	1.1 l.
Eire	200 or	50 or	250 g.	1 l. and	2 l.
N. Zealand	200 or	50 or	250 g	1.1 l. and	4.5 l.
S. Africa	400 and	50 and	250 g.	1 l. and	2 l.
U.S.A.	200 and	100 and	**	1 l. or	1 l.

* For non-European residents. (For residents of the Irish Republic or of the U.K. returning from the Channel Islands: 200 cigarettes, 50 cigars, 250 g. tobacco.)
** A reasonable quantity.

Currency restrictions. There's no limit on the amount of pounds or foreign currency you can bring into or take out of Great Britain. Check to see whether your own country has any regulations on import and export of currency.

D **DRIVING IN THE CHANNEL ISLANDS.** Whether you drive your own car to the islands by ferry or rent one when you arrive, you'll appreciate the mobility that driving in Jersey and Guernsey permits. The only other Channel Island permitting cars, Alderney, is so small that the benefit is less pronounced; and there are no car-ferry connections.

Driving conditions. At the height of the tourist season, the biggest and 118 most populous island, Jersey, suffers the kind of traffic problems you were hoping to forget. In St. Helier parking space is so precious that even the multi-storey car-parks post "no vacancy" signs. And lengthy queues at intersections are part of the local colour. Fortunately, the traffic can spread out over more than 500 miles of road, and tranquillity may be found only a few minutes from the capital on delightful country lanes.

Guernsey is less crowded but its back roads are narrow, so momentary hold-ups are inevitable. Guernsey drivers, who have boundless patience, almost never sound their horns in annoyance when a tourist stops to look for a road sign. Most road signs, if they exist at all, are hard to find or read, so some confusion ensues; even commercial attractions post understated signs. On winding country roads drivers must be alert for animals, cyclists and hikers.

Alderney has wide-open roads, well paved and with little traffic.

On all three islands traffic drives on the left in the British manner, despite the efforts of the World War II German occupation forces to change this ancient tradition.

Particularities. A yellow line painted across a road means "give way" to traffic at the intersection. In Guernsey and Alderney a large yellow arrow painted in the road does *not* mean one-way traffic but indicates that a "give way" intersection is about 30 yards away. A yellow line painted along the kerb signals a no-parking or no-stopping zone; the prohibitions are valid day and night. A "Filter in Turn" sign at a busy intersection means cars must alternate with those coming from other directions. It is generally forbidden to drive on a beach, or park on a slipway. In Guernsey, petrol stations are closed on Sunday.

Speed limits. In Jersey the all-island limit is 40 miles per hour, but in certain zones this is cut to 20 m.p.h. Guernsey's speed limit is 35 m.p.h. but some roads are signposted 25 m.p.h. or less. Alderney's 35 m.p.h. limit is cut to 20 m.p.h. in St. Anne and a racy 12 m.p.h. on the town's main street. In all three islands local drivers have been known to give way to frustration at the highway limits and open up their throttles on straight stretches of road.

Parking. In Jersey, several multi-storey car-parks attempt to solve the congestion in St. Helier. There is no charge from 6 p.m. to 8 a.m. Except where parking meters are installed, street parking requires placing a time disc in the windscreen showing when you arrived; car hire companies routinely supply them. In Guernsey, disc parking is obligatory at all times in St. Peter Port, where the unsightly scenery of car-park buildings has thus far been avoided, but parking can be difficult.

D **Fuel and oil.** Petrol is sold by the litre. Prices are higher in Alderney due to the cost of transshipment.

E **ELECTRIC CURRENT.** As in the U.K., current is 240 volts A.C. Jersey gets its electricity by undersea cable from France; it's cheaper than generating its own power.

EMERGENCIES. As in the U.K., the number to dial for police, fire, ambulance or sea rescue is **999**. The only exception is tiny Herm island, where you should dial "O" for the operator in case of emergency.

H **HAIRDRESSERS.** Competent hairdressers and barbers may be found in all the Channel Islands. There are unisex salons as well as the old-fashioned segregated mens' barbershops. As everywhere else, the more stylish the shop the higher the prices.

HOURS

Banks generally are open from 9.30 a.m. to 3.30 p.m., Monday to Friday (but in Alderney they close for lunch). Certain banks stay open later, or work Saturday mornings as well.

Museums, castles and historic sites are usually open from 9.30 or 10 a.m. to 5 or 6 p.m. during the summer. Off-season many tourist attractions operate on a severely reduced schedule. At any time of year it's wise to check with the tourist office before venturing forth.

Offices and businesses operate from about 9 a.m. to 5 or 5.30 p.m., often closing for lunch between 12.30 and 2 p.m.

Post offices. Main post offices are open from 9 a.m. to 5.30 p.m., Monday to Friday, and half a day Saturday. Sub-post offices follow the same program except that they emulate the local shops in closing early one day of the week.

Pubs. Jersey claims to enjoy the longest licensing hours in the British Isles. The intricacies could drive anyone to drink, but here, in general, are the hours you can expect to find pubs open in summer on the main islands. *Jersey.* 9 a.m. to 11 p.m. weekdays, 11 a.m. to 1 p.m. and 4.30 to 11 p.m. Sunday. *Guernsey:* 10.30 a.m. to 11 p.m. weekdays, closed all day Sunday. *Alderney:* 11 a.m. to 2 p.m. and 5 p.m. to midnight weekdays, 12 to 2 p.m. and 8 to 12 p.m. Sunday.

Shops are open between 9 a.m. and 5.30 p.m. except for early closing on Thursday in Jersey and Guernsey, Wednesday in Alderney. Lunchtime closing is standard in Alderney, less universal in the bigger islands. In the summer season, in Jersey particularly, many shops aimed at tourists stay open into the evening.

Tourist information offices. Jersey's main tourist information point, on the St. Helier waterfront, operates from 8 a.m. to 9.30 p.m. in the summer (except Sundays, 9 a.m. to noon and 7 to 9.30 p.m.) with normal office hours the rest of the year. Guernsey's tourist office in the harbour of St. Peter Port is open from 9 a.m. to 7 p.m. daily and 10 a.m. to noon and 6 to 7 p.m. Sunday. (Alderney is too small to have a walk-in office answering tourist queries.)

LANGUAGE. English is spoken in all the Channel Islands, though the older citizens of Jersey, Guernsey and Sark communicate among themselves in the local patois based on Norman French. There are significant differences among the three versions—Jersiais, Guernesiais and Sercqais. Most place-names may be traced to Norman French, and street signs are usually bilingual, giving the traditional French version and the contemporary English name (not a translation). French visitors find the patois incomprehensible, but they encounter many islanders who can speak proper French.

LAUNDRY and DRY CLEANING. Many hotels accept laundry and dry cleaning, offering speedy, if sometimes expensive, service. There are launderettes and express cleaning establishments in the towns.

MAPS. All the tourist offices give away island maps or sell them at token price. Bookshops sell more detailed maps, the most complete being the locally-produced Perry's Guide Maps booklets. The maps in this book were provided by Falk-Verlag of Hamburg.

MEDICAL CARE and HEALTH. Since all Channel Islands doctors are in private practice, visitors are advised to sign up for health insurance to cover any possible private consultation and prescription fees. However, Jersey runs a special free medical service for visitors. The General Hospital in Gloucester Street, St. Helier, provides a morning medical clinic with free advice and treatment for visitors (prescription charges extra), Monday to Friday from 9 a.m. to noon and Saturdays from 10 to 11.30 a.m. Under a reciprocal agreement with the

M National Health Service, hospital in-patient treatment in Jersey, Guernsey and Alderney is free of charge to visitors from the United Kingdom. Emergencies, of course, are dealt with around the clock, but none of the chemist's shops stay open all night.

The only particular health problem menacing visitors to the Channel Islands is the summer sun. In the absence of air pollution, the ultraviolet rays penetrate at full force, and a lobster-hued sunburn can develop almost before you notice it.

MEETING PEOPLE. The Channel Islanders are known for their helpful attitude toward strangers. They tend to be congenial, and it's easy to strike up a conversation in a pub or on the beach. In the old-fashioned British way, courtesies are an important part of daily life; "good morning", "thank you" and similar politenesses are always appreciated.

MONEY MATTERS

Currency. The Channel Islands are linked with the United Kingdom in a monetary union, but the bailiwicks of Jersey and Guernsey each issue their own banknotes and coins. They come in the standard British denominations: banknotes: £1, 5, 10, 20 and 50; coins: 1, 2, 5, 10, 20, 50p and £1. English and Scottish currencies also circulate freely, but Irish money is not accepted at face value. Before you leave the islands be certain to trade in your local currency for British money, as Channel Islands banknotes—however fascinating to collectors—are not accepted elsewhere as legal tender.

Banks and currency exchange. There are more banks in the Channel Islands than in some famous financial centres, but many of them are devoted to international high finance and have no dealings with the public. The familiar British high street banks, though, are well represented and offer a range of consumer services, including foreign exchange transactions.

Credit cards are accepted in hotels, restaurants and shops displaying the symbols of the various card companies. **Traveller's cheques** are widely accepted; cheques in foreign denominations should be cashed at the bank, where the rate is likely to be more favourable than in your hotel or restaurant.

Value Added Tax does not exist in the Channel Islands. This, and the low duty on imported luxury items, accounts for the cheaper prices on **122** many goods and services.

NEWSPAPERS and MAGAZINES. The main islands have daily papers —the Jersey *Evening Post* and the Guernsey *Evening Press*. Alderney's local news comes out biweekly in the Alderney *Journal*. Free tourist papers, handed out to arriving passengers at the airports and seaports of Jersey and Guernsey, contain calendars of events, feature articles and advertising aimed at visitors. Weather permitting, all the British national daily and Sunday newspapers arrive by air on the day of publication. In addition, the main newsagents also sell the *International Herald Tribune*, edited in Paris, as well as daily papers from France, Italy, West Germany and the Netherlands. Magazines from Britain, the U.S. and the principal European countries are also available.

PETS. Because of the danger of importing rabies, it is strictly forbidden to bring animals to the Channel Islands from anywhere except Great Britain, Northern Ireland, the Irish Republic and the Isle of Man. The prohibition applies to pets owned by British yachtsmen if they have landed at a continental port on the way to the islands. When apprehended, pet smugglers are subject to heavy fines and jail sentences.

POLICE. Island policemen wear uniforms similar to those of British bobbies, and they are just as helpful to visitors. An unexpected glamour has overtaken the Jersey police force thanks to a British TV thriller series, *Bergerac*. In real life the professional detectives are aided by an age-old network of honorary parish policemen with titles like *Centeniers* and *Vingteniers*.

PUBLIC HOLIDAYS. The Channel Islands observe the same legal holidays as the United Kingdom plus one more—May 9, Liberation Day, commemorating the capitulation of the German occupation forces in l945. The rundown:

January 1	New Year's Day
May 9	Liberation Day (except Alderney)
December 25	Christmas Day
December 26	Boxing Day
Movable dates:	
March or April	Good Friday and Easter Monday
May	Spring Bank Holidays (2)
August	Summer Bank Holiday

R **RADIO and TV.** Jersey and Guernsey each have local BBC radio stations. Other BBC radio services are either relayed by island transmitters or may be picked up directly from the "mainland". French and other continental radio stations may be heard on any transistor.

All four British TV channels are relayed by local transmitters; locally originated news and feature programmes appear on ITV's Channel Television. Special adjustments are required to receive French television programmes.

RELIGIOUS SERVICES. Each of the parishes has a Parish Church belonging to the established Anglican Church. Methodist and Roman Catholic churches are also found in many parishes. Other churches represented in the Channel Islands include Baptist, Christian Scientist, Evangelical, Jehovah's Witnesses, Mormon, Pentecostal, Quaker, Salvation Army and United Reform.

T **TIME DIFFERENCES.** Like the United Kingdom, the Channel Islands are on Greenwich Mean Time, but Summer Time moves the clock one hour forward between April and October.

Summer time differences				
New York	**Channel/UK**	Jo'burg	Sydney	Auckland
7 a.m.	**noon**	1 p.m.	9 p.m.	11 p.m.

TIPPING. In some restaurants a 10% service charge is added to the bill. If not, a 10% tip is appropriate. As in the U.K., bartenders should not be tipped, but they do accept offers of drinks. If your hotel has a concierge he should be tipped for any special services, as they occur. See the chart below for a further thumb-nail guide.

Hotel porter, per bag	20 p
Hotel maid, per day	£1
Hairdresser	10%
Taxi driver	10%
Coach tour driver	50 p

TOILETS. As in Britain, public conveniences are widely available in the Channel Islands, well maintained and easy to find. Look for the signs "Public conveniences", "WC" or male and female symbols.

TOURIST INFORMATION. There is no such thing as a Channel Islands tourist office, for each bailiwick operates its own information service. Only Jersey has an office in London:

Jersey Tourism Office, 35 Albemarle Street, London, W1X 3FB, tel. (01) 493-5278.

Or enquiries may be directed to the tourist office on the spot in Jersey:

States Tourism Committee, Weighbridge, St. Helier, Jersey, C.I., tel. (0534) 78000.

Guernsey tourist information may be obtained from:

States Tourist Board, P.O. Box 23, Guernsey, C.I., tel. (0481) 23552.

Alderney tourist information may be obtained from:

States Tourist Office, Alderney, C.I., tel. (0481)(82) 2994.

Abroad, Jersey maintains a tourist information office at 19 Blvd. Malesherbes, 75008 Paris, tel. 742-9368.

Elsewhere overseas, principal offices of the British Tourist Authority can deal with Channel Islands enquiries. Among them:

Australia   171 Clarence St., Sydney NSW 2000, tel. 298-627.

Canada   Suite 600, 94 Cumberland Street, Toronto, Ont. M5R 3N3, tel. (416) 925-6326.
Suite 451, 409 Granville Street, Vancouver, B.C. VC6 1T2, tel. (604) 669-2414.

U.S.A.   40 West 57th Street, New York, N.Y. 10019, tel. (212) 518-4700.
612 South Flower Street, Los Angeles, CA 90017, tel. (213) 623-8196.
John Hancock Center (Suite 3320), 875 North Michigan Avenue, Chicago, IL 60611, tel. (312) 787-0490.
Plaza of the Americas, North Tower, Suite 750, Dallas, TX 75201, tel. (214) 720-4040.

TRANSPORT. The most convenient way to get around each of the major islands is by car. However, there are economical public transport alternatives.

T **Buses:** All Jersey's bus lines radiate from the central bus and coach station at the Weighbridge, St. Helier. If you're planning to use the buses several times, it's worth buying a book of timetables; otherwise, consult the posted schedules. In the other bailiwick, Guernseybus, the local bus company, serves all parts of the island from the terminal in St. Peter Port. In both islands the buses tend to be historical relics, but they run to schedule. Pay the driver as you get on board. In Alderney a basic bus service operates in summer only, linking St. Anne with the beaches.

Taxis: All kinds of cars serve as taxis on the islands, from the latest luxury saloons to retired black London cabs. Taxi stands are found at the ports, airports, and in various population centres; or taxis may be ordered by telephone (numbers in the Yellow Pages of the telephone directory). The metered taxis of Jersey and Guernsey have "taxi" signs on the roof, illuminated when they are for hire. Fares, including any possible extra charges, are displayed on the meters. Supplements are charged for, among other things, waiting time, overnight hours, public holidays, baggage and additional passengers. With cars forbidden on Sark, horse-carriages are the only available transport.

Train: The only railway still operating in the Channel Islands is the line built in the 19th century to carry granite from the quarry to the harbour in Alderney. Though serving no practical purpose as a commuter line, it has been revived as a tourist attraction.

Inter-island transport: Hydrofoils are the fastest sea transport linking Jersey, Guernsey, Alderney, Sark and Herm. Fast catamarans also operate on certain routes. Small commuter planes provide frequent, fast inter-island flights between Jersey, Guernsey and Alderney.

W **WATER.** Unless otherwise signposted, water can be safely drunk from the tap anywhere in the Channel Islands.

WEIGHTS AND MEASURES. As in Britain, the metric system is beginning to make inroads in the Channel Islands. The temperature is calibrated in Celsius, not Fahrenheit, and petrol is sold by the litre. But the familiar pint of beer is unassailable, and road distances are still measured in miles.

The traditional system of land measurement, still in use, is a vestige of Norman times. It could scarcely be more confusing: a *vergée* in Jersey measures 2,151 square yards, but in Guernsey a *vergée* equals 1,960 square yards.